ADVANCE PRAISE

"The stories are great and the principles, if applied, are guaranteed to help you succeed."

—**Jack Canfield**
Co–author of *Chicken Soup for the Soul®* and *The Success Principles™*

"Congratulations on capturing the focus, fundamentals and fun in the building blocks of success. These 13 principles will enhance the reader's knowledge and inspire their journey on the road to personal achievement."

—**Dave & Beverly Savula**
Pre-Paid Legal Services, Inc.

"TJ, you have written a living classic. It is a symphony of success set to words."

—**Charles "Tremendous" Jones**
Author of *Life is Tremendous*

"This book is a compelling and winning case against mediocrity, convincing us that our dreams are possible when we are fiercely determined and make that life–changing shift from interest and desire to real commitment."

—**Keith D. Harrell**
Author of *Attitude Is Everything*

"*If You Think You Can!* is an entertaining, inspiring, and fulfilling read that gives 13 simple rules for personal achievement. If you follow TJ's advice, and who wouldn't after reading his compelling book, the sky is the limit on what you will achieve."

—Hap Klopp

Author of *The Adventure of Leadership*
and founder of the North Face

"Your success in life and work will be guaranteed when you apply these 13 laws to everything you do."

—Brian Tracy

Author of *Getting Rich Your Own Way*

"Your passion is evident throughout. If readers follow your guidelines, they will be assured of reaching higher levels of performance and happiness!"

—Bob Moawad

Chairman and founder of Edge Learning Institute, Inc.

"A must read for anyone committed to success. *If You Think You Can!* clearly articulates the fundamental principles that have made me a self-made millionaire. For anyone, seeking unlimited success this is the book for you."

—Dean Kosage

World Wide International

"TJ clearly outlines the important steps necessary to achieve great success and enrich your personal and professional life. This book is a goldmine of information on personal development."

—Nido R. Qubein

Chairman of Great Harvest Bread Company
and founder of the *National Speakers Association Foundation*

"People often ask me for advice on how to find success; now I will simply give them two words—TJ Hoisington!"

—Troy Dunn

Celebrity guest and author

"Great book! This is one of the most practical books ever written on the art of achievement. It clearly shows you the fundamentals to getting whatever you want in any area of life."

—Wayne Allyn Root

Host of *Wayne Allyn Root's WinningEDGE* on Spike TV and author of *The Zen of Gambling*

"As I was reading over some of the Laws of Achievement that TJ covers in his new book, I found myself going – "Focus, yep... Urgency, that's right... Developing a Winning Perspective, right on... Master Your Thinking, oh yeah... The Power Of Decisions, good one..." and on and on... TJ is right on point in sharing what it takes to reach the top in your chosen field of endeavor. This one is a keeper. Go, Go, Go!!!"

—Jerry "DRhino" Clark

www. clubrhino. net

"TJ Hoisington has discovered life's ultimate success principles—read this book and change your life forever!"

—Patrick Snow

Best-selling author of *Creating Your Own Destiny*

"If You Think You Can! is an easy read with a powerful message for those who are willing to invest in themselves. It provides the rules needed to reach your full potential."

—Ernest A. Parada

Director, Combat Sustainment Wing

Hill AFB, Utah

"I have known TJ for many years. I have watched him apply the principles he teaches in this book. His business and career have expanded exponentially as a result. If you follow his advice your goals and dreams *WILL* come true. TJ walks his talk."

—Eric Lofholm

President of Eric Lofholm International, Inc.

"If there is something you want to achieve, then this is the book for you. TJ has made the principles that lead to extraordinary achievement inspiring and easy to understand."

—Orrin Hudson

www. Besomeone. org

If You THINK *You* CAN!

Thirteen Laws that Govern the Performance of High Achievers

TJ HOISINGTON

MANJUL

Manjul Publishing House

First published in India by

MANJUL

Manjul Publishing House Pvt. Ltd.

Corporate Office:

2nd Floor, Usha Preet Complex,
42 Malviya Nagar, Bhopal 462 003 - India
E-mail: manjul@manjulindia.com
Website: www.manjulindia.com

Marketing Office:

7/32, Ground Floor, Ansari Road, Daryaganj,
New Delhi 110 002
Email: booksupplyco@gmail.com

This edition first published in 2005
Sixth impression 2012

ISBN 978-81-8322-115-3

Printed & bound in India by Thomson Press (India)Ltd.

To my best friend in the entire world—my lovely wife, Danielle, who continues to believe in me and support me through thick and thin.

We are all living in cages with the doors wide open.

— GEORGE LUCAS

CONTENTS

FORWARD

by

Harland C. Stonecipher

Over the past thirty years numerous authors have approached me to endorse their books. In fact, I am contacted on a regular basis by people who want me to provide their books or training programs to our Pre-Paid Legal Services, Inc. associates around the world. Over the years I have been very cautious in doing this and as a result I have only recommended a few books, over a thirty-year period.

If You Think You Can: Thirteen Laws that Govern the Performance of High Achievers is a book I can recommend. Not only is it an enjoyable read, but also it covers the fundamental principles that will help anyone succeed.

I personally believe applying the principles outlined in this book will help people achieve their goals and dreams.

The author mentions in this book that just as there are laws that govern nature there are also laws that govern achievement. TJ Hoisington has packed a lot of great information in this simple and concise book. For anyone seeking success at any level I invite you to read this book and make it a part of your personal library.

PREFACE

I HAVE ALWAYS BEEN FASCINATED BY achievement. This fascination has led me to study its laws and principles in depth. In fact, half of my life has been devoted to better understanding this phenomenon.

As I travel the country speaking to audiences of all kinds, I have come to realize that many people set out unequipped to achieve. Just as there are certain laws that govern nature, there are laws that govern performance and achievement. Unfortunately, either people are unaware of them, and therefore don't align themselves accordingly, or they simply do not apply them. As a result, many people chase after goals and find that the results they desire constantly elude them.

For this reason, I have written this book. It is filled with rich and moving stories of both successes and failures. It is also filled with true principles and insights that, when applied, will help you achieve whatever you desire.

As part of my research, I went back to some of the classic books and greatest writings of all time. I studied the greatest achievers and discovered what made them great and what helped them to obtain their desired results. Then I made those distinctions easy for all people to understand and embrace. I have also used some of my own successes and failures to illustrate the applicability of these ageless principles. However, I have purposely limited the number of personal stories because of my desire to share some of the classic examples that have inspired millions of people. The power is in the principles!

In my research I have found that there are thirteen fundamental laws or principles that govern achievement. We live in a time where self–help and finding fulfillment seems to dominate the bookshelves, yet I have specifically written about the art of achievement. If there is something you want to achieve, this is the book for you.

The purpose of this book is to remind people what *is* possible and *how* it is possible. As they read this short and concise book, readers will have frequent and powerful "aha" moments. There is an old saying, "When the student is ready, the teacher will appear." These pages are filled with powerful stories and examples that will move and inspire you to take action and make these time–tested principles work in your life.

It is my intention to be inclusive of both men and women; however, in order to be concise, I will use words such as "he, men, man," etc. Please know that I am referring to both genders—men and women.

CHAPTER 1

The Greatness Within You

ONCE UPON A TIME THERE WERE DREAMS. Dreams of greatness. A time when we wanted to be somebody. A time when we wanted to achieve something, to get somewhere. Unfortunately, along the way, millions have forgotten that we are the masters of our own fate and creators of our own destiny. As time passes, many have given up on the idea that big dreams and goals are achievable. Far too many have lost sight of the greatness we possess within.

In 1957, members of a Thailand monastery were put in charge of moving a large clay statue of Buddha to a new location. As the crane lifted the statue, the weight was so great that the statue began to crack. Worse yet, it started to rain. In fear of seriously damaging the statue, they lowered it, placed a tarp over it, and decided to continue the following morning. That night, while one of the monks was inspecting the statue with a flashlight, he noticed a reflection shining from out of a crack that was forming in the clay. Out of curiosity he retrieved a hammer and chisel, and started chipping away. Finally, after much of the clay had been removed, he realized that it was not a clay statue at all, but rather a large, solid-gold Buddha.

Many historians believe that several hundred years earlier, the Thai monks had covered the golden Buddha with clay in an effort to disguise it from the Burmese army. A battle ensued and consequently the Thai monks were destroyed, and it wasn't until 1957 that the true nature of the Buddha was discovered. Today, the golden Buddha rests in a temple in Thailand, open to the public to see.

Like the Buddha, we all have great potential and untold wealth within. Yet, due to the battles of life, we too find it difficult to see beyond our own layers of clay.

Some years ago Converse promoted this ad: "Champions are born and then unmade." The ad implied that the innate greatness we possessed the moment we came out of the womb would soon be replaced with limitations and defeat. We were born to win, yet soon we are conditioned to lose.

Starting in childhood, conditioning is a gradual, yet consistent and relentless progression. The average fourth-grade child has heard the words, "No, you *can't* do that" over seventy thousand times! Unfortunately, for many this is just the beginning of the destructive conditioning that will be pounded into their heads for years to come. Buck Minister Fuller put it this way, "All children are born geniuses; 9,999 out of every 10,000 are swiftly, inadvertently degeniusized by grown-ups."

Even as we get older we make settlements—settling for less than our true potential—as a result of what someone said or did. Maybe we had a goal, and out of our excitement we shared the goal with someone we admired only to hear them say, "You are going to do *what?*" "You can't do that." "You've never done something like that before." "You don't have the education, money, talent, etc." They questioned our abilities, and in that vulnerable moment, we believed them.

In his book *Love and Awakening*, John Welwood uses the analogy of a castle to illustrate this conditioning process. Imagine being a magnificent castle with thousands of rooms. Each room is elegant, even perfect. You love each room for its uniqueness, how magnificent it is, and for its character. Then imagine one day someone coming into one of your rooms and boldly telling you that the room was ugly, worthless, or unacceptable. Consequently, out of your need to be loved and accepted, you found yourself closing the room off from the rest of the world. Then imagine if most everyone else who entered your castle over a period of time also thought that many of your rooms were imperfect and needed to be changed. One after another, slowly but surely, imagine each door being closed. Eventually, you realize that by closing off these parts of you—your castle, or your dreams, that it actually started making you feel safe. Soon you found yourself living in a castle with a thousand rooms—occupying only one or two.

Many are guided by the limiting belief that high achievers simply have superior talents and that is why they are successful. Well, research indicates that in most cases the opposite is true. After a five-year study of 120 of the top artist's, athletes, and scholars, Dr. Benjamin Bloom and his research team determined that success was more about "drive and determination, not great natural talent." In fact, the belief that they were special surfaced long before any signs of greatness or talent were noticed. Dr. Bloom went on to say that even the mothers of those studied said, "It was their other child [brother or sister] who had the greater gift." As the saying goes, "Sometimes those who are given more end up with less, and those who are given less end up with more." Maybe you have noticed at times that the more talent someone has, the lazier they are. I'm going to show you throughout this book that regardless of whether or not you possess talent or any other special advantage, your dreams are possible.

This was the case with Will Kellogg, who was reported to be a shy man with few friends, limited interests, and no discernible talents. Will was forty-six years of age before he made the decision to go into business for himself. At the time he was working for his older brother, Dr. Kellogg, who never paid Will more than $87 in a month.

One day, while Will and Dr. Kellogg were experimenting to improve the food for his patients, they discovered "flakes" by accident. Will had left a pot of boiling wheat to stand a little too long. When the wheat became tempered, he rolled it into a flake. Will tried convincing his brother to mass-market the discovery, but Dr. Kellogg refused. He doubted Will's idea. As a result, in 1906 Will decided to market the idea on his own and he became one of the richest men in America.

Many are tempted to set their dreams or goals aside before they make the slightest effort to achieve them because of fear. What do they fear? They fear the unknown, failure, what others will think, and they even fear success. As a result, many find themselves living what Henry David Thoreau describes as "lives of quiet desperation." Others unconsciously allow past failures to determine their future. They unceasingly re-live their past attempts and failures. They think because it didn't work out then, it probably won't work out now.

It is easy to find reasons why things won't work. The entire world is full of rationales as to why you can't be great. Achievers, however, find the reasons why things will work. For centuries people commonly believed that the earth was at the center of the universe and that the sun revolved around it. Although many great minds disputed this belief, it wasn't until Galileo came along and proved otherwise. In order to do so, he took the leaders of that time to the tower of San Marco, and with his newly perfected telescope, he showed them his discovery. It threatened the leaders of that day because it contradicted their strongly held beliefs. The leaders became angry and even tortured Galileo in an effort to get him to retract his position. Eventually he did just that in February, 1633. Out of fear for his life, he retracted his beliefs.

Like the leaders during the time of Galileo, people who can't see new possibilities for themselves are likely unable to see new possibilities for you. People are certain they know what's best for you and often conclude you don't have what it takes. They will try their hardest to prevent you from taking the leap. If you are not careful, you too could be pressured into retracting your own beliefs and dreams.

There's a crucial time when you need to tune out the critics and a time when you must cease from seeking their approval. Cavett Robert said that there are many people who don't want to take the trip themselves, yet pose as experts who criticize the travels of others. These are not the people with whom you want to associate—they are toxic.

There is also a time when you must stop worrying what others think and start thinking for yourself and your own dreams. I like Dr. Daniel Amen's 18/40/60 rule: When you are 18, you worry about what others are thinking of you; when you are 40 you don't give a darn what others think of you; when you are 60 you realize that nobody has been thinking of you at all. Did you get that? People aren't sitting around thinking about you. Most people are spending most of their time thinking about themselves; their own problems, challenges, and opportunities. Begin today by investing your time thinking about your own dreams and future that desperately awaits your arrival—and stop worrying about what others are thinking!

The truth is, you are powerful beyond measure, even though there is a part of you that would have you believe otherwise. When the pressure is on, there lies in all of us the temptation to compromise for being average and to live a life of mediocrity—to take the path of least resistance and go along with the crowd. We may ask ourselves whether or not we really do have what it takes to achieve our dreams. In their book, *I Want to Change, but I Don't Know How*, Tom Rusk and Randy Read eloquently relate that people frequently go through life playing it safe. Why? Because it gives them the permission to believe, "If I never let myself feel too good, maybe I'll never get hurt too badly."

Gandhi, Grandma Moses, Steven Spielberg, Rosa Parks, Steve Jobs, and Oprah Winfrey; each of these individuals stand as examples of what is possible. They have managed to break the rules, stretch the limits, and even make history. This, however, begs the questions: If they can do it . . . why not you? What about your greatness? You have it, but have you tapped into it? If so, how much? How can you draw on more of your greatness and begin living your dreams and achieving your goals?

Although inspired by greatness, we sometimes doubt our own potential. Maybe we know that something is possible, but we just aren't confident that it is possible for ourselves, given our current abilities or our past. We think, "I don't have any special talents." "I don't have what they have." "I could never do that." Stop! You must come to grips with the fact that within you exists the same powerful abilities that enable winners to be winners—you simply must choose to apply them. There comes a time when you must re-enter your castle rooms that you have closed off from the rest of the world and pull up the blinds and open the windows, allowing fresh air and light to enter in. Decide you are going to defy the odds. Decide that you are going to start achieving more.

Extraordinary people are simply ordinary people that do extra ordinary things. Many of them did not have the education, talent, resources or other special advantages. All of them had fears and insecurities. Oprah Winfrey came from a dysfunctional and abusive childhood. Einstein didn't speak until he was four years old. His teacher described him as "mentally slow, unsociable, and adrift forever in his foolish dreams." Others were in debt to the hilt. Thomas Edison only had three months of formal education. William Lear, the creator of Lear Jet Corporation, dropped out of school in the sixth grade. Yet, each of these achievers and many more have gone on to become great successes. In fact, did you know that 20% of America's millionaires never set foot in college? Did you know that 21 of the 222 Americans listed as billionaires in 2003 never got their college diplomas and two of them never finished high school? So although learning and personal growth is essential for success, a formal degree is not a requirement. *The most important ingredient that determines whether or not a person succeeds is the power of believing in yourself.* This is the common ingredient that is unquestionably weaved among all achievers. Nothing is more important than first having a belief in yourself.

I call belief, "the embryo of possibility." It is in belief that dreams are formed. Likewise, it is the result of a belief that leads one to take the necessary action that will turn their dreams into reality. Even if you find yourself in undesirable circumstances, it is the power of your beliefs that enable you to change your response to the circumstances, thus changing your overall experience. Belief in ourselves truly is the driving force that determines our destiny.

Ultimately, it is not the external circumstances or conditions that limit you. It is you! It is your negative thoughts, comfort zones, self-defeating habits, poor strategies, blame lists, or even your failure to continuously educate yourself and grow. You are the greatest obstacle in life that prevents you from going from where you are, to where you want to be. The moment you realize and decide that you are the single most determining factor as to whether or not you succeed or fail, only then will your life have a chance to improve.

The wonderful part of all this is that you can change. You can grow. You can rise above your challenges and start producing the results you desire. No matter how difficult your circumstances may seem at this moment, possibilities are still available to you. Carl Joseph was born with one leg. Not using crutches or artificial legs, he decided to play football in high school. He worked so hard that eventually he made All-State defensive lineman. The local newspapers said, "He ran so smoothly and so effortlessly that when you watched him run you could hardly tell he was missing a leg. Especially when he was chasing down the quarterback from behind." In basketball he could dunk the ball, and in track he could jump five feet ten inches—all with one leg. In fact, even with his disadvantage, he went on to receive a four-year athletic training scholarship from the University of Pittsburgh. He said, "It is all in the mind. My mind always told me that I could do things, and I just went and did them. I never worried that I couldn't do something, I just did it. You just keep trying, and you will always get there." Despite an apparent limitation, what enabled Carl to go for it? What secret did he possess when others would have given up? What specific habits did he form that made dunking a basketball or receiving a full-ride scholarship possible? Continue reading—the answers will be shared throughout this book!

I have also discovered many people who quietly excuse their lack of achieving by convincing themselves that they are too young and inexperienced. I too found myself giving in to this way of thinking and it has accounted for numerous opportunities on which I neglected to act. I also notice others, who were once convincing themselves that they were too young to achieve a particular goal and now they are convincing themselves they are too old. The fact is, neither is true! Age is not a prerequisite for success.

For instance, actors Matt Damon and Ben Affleck were eleven years old when they found a quiet area in the school cafeteria and held meetings to talk about their latest acting projects. At fifteen years old, George Parker created one of the most successful games ever produced—Monopoly. What were the success habits that led two young men to create the internet search engine, Google–and turn it into a billion-dollar success? What secret did these young men possess that enabled them to create enormous success at such a young age?

At the other end of the age spectrum, what about people like Jack Welch, Donald Trump, Sam Walton, or Dave Thomas of Wendy's fast-food restaurants? What habits did they possess that led to their success? Whether young or old, goals are attainable.

Norman MaClean, was seventy-three years old and rejected the idea of retirement. Having taught literature at the University of Chicago for thirty years, he still felt something tugging at him. He wondered if he too could be a writer, so he went to his cabin in Montana and spent the next two years writing. At the end of this time, his writings were published in a book called *A River Runs Through It*, which eventually became a movie.

When it comes to age, George Eliot said, "It is never too late to be what you might have been." Anna Mary Robertson Moses began sketching at a very young age. Intrigued by every little detail, she began using berries to bring more color into her paintings. As life would have it, she was forced to put her paintings on hold because of the demand of farming life. For sixty years she didn't paint at all. Finally, in 1938 she retired from farming and once again took up painting. By the time of her death, twenty-three years later, she had painted thousands of scenes remembered from her childhood and became known around the world as Grandma Moses. What was the unique formula that led Grandma Moses to leave such a lasting legacy? What was the secret of Norman MaClean? Is there something they understood that others didn't?

I don't know your age or what your current circumstances look like. I don't know what your past was like, and I definitely don't know what the future holds for you. You are the only person who can make that determination. Here, however, is what I do know: Your past does not have to equal your future. You can decide today to change your life by simply putting into action the principles in this book. You can decide that you deserve more. Stephen Covey said, "Deep within each one of us there is an inner longing to lead a life of greatness and contribution, to really matter and to really make a difference."

J.K. Rowling understood the principles outlined in this book, even if she wasn't consciously aware of them. She dealt with poverty, unemployment, and being a single mother, yet stayed true to her personal vision. At one point life was so difficult that she went on welfare, and made only $105 per week. It was reported that in an effort to save every penny, she cut back on meals and spent all day in local cafes in an attempt to save on her heating bill at home. At the cafes she would write on note pads while her daughter Jessica napped beside her.

Although Rowling experienced severe episodes of depression, she was determined to complete her book and have it accepted. After waiting three years for a response, she finally published her book and the Harry Potter phenomenon began. Since then, over 250 million of her books have been sold worldwide and Rowling was named the world's best-paid author of all time—with her worth reaching over one billion dollars. J.K. Rowling knew what it would take to turn her dream into reality. Do you?

Oliver Wendell Holmes said, "What lies behind us and what lies before us are tiny matters compared to what lies within us." I'm presuming that you are reading this book because you believe in what's possible or you have the desire to believe in what's possible. Maybe you are reading this book to maintain the competitive edge. Maybe you're searching for that one idea or distinction that will change your life, or simply give you the slight edge beyond where you were yesterday. It's likely you want a book that will be a source of inspiration for you, a friend, or your organization. If any of the above are true, then you are reading the right book.

Like the laws of nature, there are laws that govern your performance, and thereby your achievement. You can either ignore these laws or you can effectively apply them to get whatever you want. Even if you are reading this book in terms of your team or organization, let me suggest that you keep in mind that the laws are universal. The laws that make up a great individual are the same laws that make up a great organization.

If you are reading this book, yet content with where you are and desire for no more than what you already have, then this book will simply serve as a enjoyable read. Hopefully, you want more. Even if it is a little more than what you currently have. Whether it's the desire for a better relationship, more time with family, better job or position, increased financial success, or greater spirituality—the principles in this book will help you achieve these goals. Remember, achieving is not merely about getting; it is about becoming all that you possibly can, and then contributing in a positive way.

I'm reminded of my first teacher who said, "Achievement is a choice of thoughts and activities." Today is your time to step up. Defy the odds. Stop seeking the approval of others and begin achieving your goals and living your dreams.

In the following pages you will learn about *thirteen laws* that govern the achievement of any goal. My advice as you read this book is to first believe in the amazing reality that dreams are possible. Goals, whether large or small, personal or organizational, are achievable. The bottom line is that *if you think you can . . . you can.*

Second, apply the time-tested laws and complete the exercises at the end of each chapter. It's your choice to not only read them, but to also apply them. Boldly and confidently put them to work, and you will experience their true merit.

CHAPTER 2

The Power of Decisions

Law #1

JUST AS GREAT POWER EXISTS WITHIN a tiny seed, explosive power resides within you, and your decisions are the means to unleashing that power. In order to turn a dream into reality, you must begin with a decision.

Unlike animals, you do not have to fall victim to a genetic code or the conditioning of your past. You don't have to allow life's circumstances to determine your destiny. If you are stuck, you don't have to remain stuck. If you are unhappy with where you are today, you can decide to change. Ralph Waldo Emerson once said, "Don't go where the path may lead, go where there is no path and leave a trail." Decisions are the force that changes your direction in a moment's notice.

Every person on the planet possesses a power called "free agency," which is the power to make decisions. We all have the freedom to decide what we want to think. We all have the power to choose our behaviors and therefore our outcomes. Some have used this freedom to choose noble endeavors while others have chosen otherwise. Whether good or bad, all achievement is the direct result of the power of decisions. Let's take a look at the enormous power that decisions can play in our lives.

It was in a moment of decision that Rosa Parks had a great impact on the Civil Rights movement. In 1955 she refused to give up her seat on a crowded bus to a white man—a decision that changed a nation. That single decision led to a series of events that moved America closer to racial equality. It reflected the explosive effect that one decision can have.

What about Lance Armstrong, the consecutive six-time Tour de France winner? At age twenty-five, cancer forced Lance to stop riding. Cancer had spread from its origin to both his lungs and brain, and he was told he wouldn't live longer than a couple years. In his autobiography, Lance recalls that he was scared and often had thoughts that he might never ride again. He even said that there were times when he felt like giving up. Even so, he made the decision to fight back, get healthy, and get on his bike again. He made the *decision* not to give in to the illness, and instead to do everything in his power to rise above the challenge. When others would have given up, Lance made the decision to press forward. Today he not only made history, but he is a world champion because of his decision to fight—and fight hard.

In stark contrast, it was a series of poor decisions that lead to the deaths of Elvis Presley, John Belushi, Kurt Cobain, and many others. It was the decisions of executives that led to the collapse of Tycoon Corporation, Enron, and others. Even when you look at the differences between Gandhi and Hitler, it was not only their ideals, but also their decisions that led to their actions that determined their place in history.

Unfortunately, we don't always recognize the impact of our decisions. Most of the time, the effect doesn't reveal itself until months or even years down the road. In fact, we all make decisions that at times seem inconsequential, yet have far-reaching outcomes.

Think for a moment about the decisions you made this morning. When you awoke, did you quickly get out of bed or did you lie there debating, in an effort to gain a few more minutes of sleep? What did you eat? Did you leave your home on a positive note, or did you rush out the door paying little attention to your family members?

When you entered your workplace, what was the first thing you did? Did you greet people with a smile? You probably didn't give those decisions much thought when you made them. However, could they potentially affect your future? Definitely! Imagine for a moment that you slept an extra thirty minutes a day. Could that eventually have a negative impact on a goal that you are working on? You bet! If you ate an unhealthy breakfast or overate, could that have an impact? Sure it could—if you made a consistent habit of it. If you made the decision in your relationships to show more love and patience, could that affect the quality of your relationships? Of course!

Again, every decision you make will either keep you on the course to achievement or lead you away from it. Rarely does a person lose a relationship overnight. It starts with one poor decision that can lead to a *series* of poor decisions. You don't simply wake up one morning having lost weight, nor do you reach the point of obesity immediately after eating. You don't become a chain smoker by smoking one cigarette. Neither do you wake up one day with all your goals achieved and living the life of your dreams.

Although these decisions may seem minor and insignificant, they illustrate the point. *Now here is where decisions really shape your destiny:* When you decide to press forward despite defeat. When you decide to take action despite your fears and worries. When you decide to maintain an empowering perspective, even when things aren't going your way. When you decide to grow a backbone and cease to be indecisive! How about making the decision to go after what you want—to go after your dreams? These are the decisions that have an explosive impact on your life.

Start right now by making a decision to stop defending your habits. Stop complaining about your circumstances and start doing something about them. Stop blaming others or your past for why you aren't achieving what you want to achieve. Make a decision to be happy from here on out. Make a decision to have higher self-esteem! Make a decision that you are a person worthy of your goals! Most importantly, make a decision to believe in yourself!

I repeat, wherever you are today is simply the result of your thoughts and beliefs. These transform into desires, which lead to *decisions*. If you want to change your life, then change your decisions. It's that simple.

Ultimately the type of decisions that will drastically improve your chances of success will be "true decisions." When a true decision is made, you cut yourself off from all other options except those to which you are committed. In his book *Think and Grow Rich*, Napoleon Hill shared a story of a general who sailed across the sea to engage in a war with another country. He knew that his men would be greatly outnumbered, and that they would need to be highly committed and motivated if they were going to win. Once his army had exited the ship with all their supplies and made it to shore, he ordered the ships to be burned. As his men watched the ships go up in flames, the general turn to them and said, "We either win or die."

The general made a true decision. In fact, the word *decision* comes from the Latin root meaning "to cut off from." And there comes a time in every person's life when making a true decision is necessary. A decision where you believe so deeply in what you want that there is no option for turning back. Yes, it will be necessary at times to change decisions along the way as it relates to your strategy, but the primary decision will not change.

Getting to the point of making a true decision takes time. Have you ever felt frustrated because you waffle on a decision? I must have tried losing weight a dozen times before I actually did it. I was once forty pounds overweight, but it wasn't until I made a definite decision that I wanted the fat gone that I lost the weight. I had to get to the point where changing my eating and exercising habits lasted more than a few days before falling back into the same old patterns. To become committed, I had to get to the point of do or die. As a result of making this true decision, I naturally and consistently began taking action that led to losing the weight in less than ninety days.

In life, once you make decisions, you must take responsibility for them. On several occasions, I have encountered people who have made poor decisions which caused challenges to enter into their lives. Often these people get discouraged and assume a victim mentality. That leads them to blame life rather than their own decisions that contributed to the problem. They forget that although they have the power to choose, they never have the power to completely choose the consequences of their choices. If we want different outcomes, we must begin making new decisions.

One of the great thieves that robs people from making true decisions is *indecision*. What causes indecision? Fear! Fear of making the wrong decision. Fear of what others will think. Fear of the unknown. Fear is the greatest of all thieves. Indecision often has a higher price to be paid than making the wrong decision. Why? Because the price is paid over the long haul in missed opportunities—the very opportunities that can help you achieve what you want.

Any decision is better than no decision. Achievers understand that they will not always make perfect decisions, but they know they can grow from the wrong ones. President Theodore Roosevelt said, "He who makes no mistakes makes no progress." Achievers see each decision and its outcome as stepping-stones toward reaching their final goal.

I once had the privilege of speaking to Charles "Tremendous" Jones. It was at a time in my life when I found myself struggling between staying at or leaving a business I had created. My desire was to live my dream, something that required a change in my direction. Although I wanted my dream, I experienced fear. "What if I make the wrong decision?" "What if I don't have what it takes?" I explained my struggle to Mr. Jones, at which point he responded, "We weren't born to make right or wrong decisions, we were born to make decisions, and then make them right."

He wasn't suggesting that you shouldn't strive to make wise decisions. There are times when calculated decisions are necessary. He also wasn't suggesting that there weren't right or wrong decisions in life, because there are. What he meant was that we know deep down what is best for us, yet we become paralyzed by fear.

William James said, "There is no more miserable human being than one in whom nothing is habitual but indecision." Making decisions requires faith and belief in others and in one's self. It requires faith that, enables us to firmly believe that, in the end, things will work out—even if the outcome is initially, slightly off course. Often, when we are unable to see the end result or unable to predict the future, we feel the safest decision is to make no decision at all.

In his book *The Adventure of Leadership*, Hap Klopp the founder of the North Face, shares the experience of an expedition that turned disastrous. He told of the Whittaker brothers, Lou and Jim, who lead the expedition. They were tall and strong men standing over six feet. While crossing a glacier in Alaska, one of the members of the expedition team fell and broke his leg. He needed medical attention immediately. They were out in the middle of nowhere on top of Mt. McKinley, and time was running out. As the sun was beginning to go down and the temperature was dropping fast, they radioed for a jet helicopter, but it was unavailable. In its place, a standard helicopter was called to perform the rescue, but it did not do well in high altitudes.

Finally, the helicopter arrived. They quickly loaded the climber into the helicopter, but the added weight of the injured man prevented the helicopter from lifting off the ground. The air was too thin at such a high altitude. As it began getting dark, the Whittakers were forced to improvise. Hap writes, "They each grabbed a rail of the helicopter and heaved it off the edge of the cliff." The Whittakers watched as the helicopter went down "like a rock through the thin air." Hap adds, "Finally, halfway down, the blades of the helicopter caught air and it flew off toward the hospital." Talk about decisions—that was a big one!

Sometime later, after the experience, Hap asks Jim Whittaker, "What if it didn't work?" Jim replied, "Sometimes you just know." Hap goes on to say, "Obstacles will inevitably pop up on the path to fulfilling your passion, and when they do, like the Whittakers, you must listen to your instinct, your intuition, that little voice deep inside that just knows."

So it is with you. You have that same instinct and intuition. That little voice deep inside you that *just knows*. So be bold, have faith, and make a decision. Make one today . . . make one now! And when you are unsure, make the best decision according to your current level of awareness and the resources you have in that moment. Regardless of the outcome, you will have greater knowledge and will be better prepared for what is to come.

In addition, when making decisions, as long as the sum total of your good decisions outweigh any poor decisions—you are moving in the right direction.

Starting today I make the true decision to: _______

____

____

CHAPTER 3

Demanding the Best from Yourself

Law #2

EVERYTHING YOU HAVE RIGHT NOW IN YOUR life is a reflection of what you expect to have, and your commitment to it. Aristotle said, "What you expect, that you shall find." In order to get what you want, you must begin expecting and demanding more out of yourself than you currently do. Just like building a muscle, you would wouldn't lift the same amount of weight indefinitely and expect muscle to grow. Instead, you would increase the weight, placing greater demand on the muscle. This in turn, would cause the muscle to expand and grow.

A number of years ago, while working for Anthony

Robbins, I learned that there was a big difference between being interested in something, and being committed to it. In life, we only get what we *must* have. If you don't *have* to *have* something, it is unlikely you will take the required action to achieve your particular goal. When a person merely is interested in a goal, rather than committed to it, they are likely to take action only when it is convenient. On the other hand, people who get what they want make it a habit to do whatever is required—whenever it is required. You can always tell between those who are interested, and those who are committed. How can you tell? Interests show up in conversation, and commitment shows up in behavior. A committed person goes from thinking, "It would be nice to have this or that" to "I must—I will—I am committed." And then they go and do!

Achievers are constantly *demanding* more from themselves compared with what the mass majority of people are accepting for themselves. Because they set a high expectation for themselves, they understand that sacrifices will be necessary for a time in order to achieve what they want. When others are relaxing or taking breaks, the achiever continues hustling. John F. Kennedy was referring to achievers when he said they "do what they must—in spite of personal consequences, in spite of obstacles, danger and pressures."

We all have the power to make things happen in

our lives. When you want something badly enough, you do whatever it takes to get it. Even children have learned this principle. When children truly want something, they become utterly unstoppable. You can tell them "no" a dozen times and they refuse to relent. Finally, they wear you out and you give in to their plea. As adults, many of us have lost this same determination. We make compromises, we rationalize and we give in to mediocrity far too easily. In fact, the most pervasive disease in the world is the disease of mediocrity.

It will not always be an easy task to achieve a desired result. It is rarely an easy walk in the park. I learned early on that if I truly wanted something, I had to go from doing "just enough" to get by, to really pushing myself. I remember in fourth grade having to be pulled out of social studies class and taken to a special reading class. I was told I was a slow reader and had poor comprehension. I can remember sitting in an extra small chair at an extra small table reading comic books. After reading, I would take a comprehension test which confirmed what I already suspected—I was not a reader and probably never would be. It was very discouraging.

I remember envying my older brother Steve who read every night before going to sleep. By age eleven he had read all the *Hardy Boys* and *Nancy Drew* books. We shared a bedroom and every night after the lights were turned off, I would ask him to share with me what he read, and he would proceed to tell me. The joy he received from reading was obvious and it inspired me.

Consequently, one day I told my mother I wanted to learn to read like Steve and asked if she would buy me a book. Mother agreed and told me she would do exactly what she did for Steve, which was to buy me my first book. She said once I had read that one, she would buy me another book. Not wanting to copy Steve by reading the *Hardy Boys* or *Nancy Drew* books, I instead chose a different book—the *Bobbsey Twins*. Excitedly, I remember lying down that first night before the lights went off as I started to read. Did I say started to read? That is an overstatement. The moment I started reading the first page I quickly realized how difficult reading was for me. It took real effort. In fact, I can remember struggling through the first page. I read it three or four times, and I still didn't understand what I had read.

That night I was again reminded that, "I must not be a reader—it's not who I am." My whole identity was shaped greatly by this belief. I also thought my brother must have been more talented than I and that a person either has it or they don't. I have since *decided* that this thought is erroneous.

Sometimes we don't change because it is easier to stay the same. In my case I didn't believe in myself and decided to give up. From that day forward, until I reached high school, I hadn't read one book cover to cover. Then one day I was in my father's bedroom when I noticed a cassette tape on his dresser. It was a copied tape that read on one side, *The Day My Life Turned Around* and on the other side, *How to Live Financially Independent.* At sixteen years old and coming from a large family with little financial means, I was intrigued by these titles.

I put the tape in my pocket and went upstairs to my bedroom that I shared with two other brothers. I put the tape in my Walkman and began listening to concepts and principles for living a successful life. I was amazed by what I was hearing. The tape inspired me so much that I listened to it at least twenty times that first month. The speaker on the tape was my "first" teacher of success principles, Jim Rohn. One of the concepts he taught on that tape was, "If you want your life to change then you must change." He said that you must not wait for your spouse, boss, taxes, or weather to change before you change. Rather, if you will change, your entire world will change. So I had my work cut out for me. He taught that achievers are readers, and I definitely wanted to be an achiever. Like so many at that age, I wanted to be somebody and get somewhere in my life.

That tape led me to many other tapes on the subject, and they all seemed to teach the same messages:

"all leaders are readers" and that you have to raise your standards and not only expect more, but demand more from yourself. I learned that all you have to do is make it a habit of becoming better than average. Even being slightly better than average can dramatically separate the achievers from the un-achievers.

Finally, the day came when I decided that I didn't want to become a victim of my inability to read. I didn't want that to stand in my way of being successful at whatever I chose. So, I saved up a few dollars and purchased my first book, *The Adventure of Leadership* by Hap Klopp. Three or four months later after struggling to read through it, I purchased my second book, *Live Your Dreams* by Les Brown. I read both from cover to cover. It was a major accomplishment for me at that time. Today I read a minimum of three to four books per month.

That decision—and my commitment to it—enabled me to turn one of my greatest weaknesses into a useful strength. By taking responsibility for my weakness, I was able to change it, which has greatly shaped who I am today.

I went from saying *it would be nice* to read to *I will* learn to read—no matter what it takes. When you make the shift from interest to commitment, only then will you hold yourself to a higher standard and begin producing results accordingly. Whatever you decide to go after, you must make an absolute commitment. If you want more out of your job, relationships, health, and life, then you must do whatever is required.

You must commit yourself to true standards, which are those that you consistently stand by, regardless of their difficulty. These standards are those which you consistently uphold even when no one else is watching.

Even when it comes to losing weight, only those who are truly committed over a period of time will see the weight disappear. Good intentions will only take you so far. In *Working with Emotional Intelligence* Daniel Goleman said, "The reason 80% of those that lose weight gain it back in one year is because they have not given up the lifestyle that supported it."

Getting what you want will require that you sacrifice whatever you want for the moment for what you want long-term. It is essential to sacrifice or postpone those things that stand in the way of you achieving your goals.

It would have been easier to decide that reading wasn't for me and pursue other goals that didn't require as much effort. However, had I accepted my fate as a non-reader, then in what other areas of my life would I have made compromises? At a young age, I unconsciously knew that if I began settling for less than my true potential, eventually this compromise could become a habit and failure could become my destiny.

It is easier to lower your standards than it is to raise them. It is easier to go along with the masses than it is to separate yourself from them. My advice is that whenever there is doubt between the easier path and the one that requires you to stretch, get in the habit of stretching. Alex Osborne once said, "Unless you are willing to go beyond that which you have already mastered, you will never grow."

As mentioned earlier, whatever you have in your life right now, is a reflection of what you *must* have. You may want more, but until it becomes a true standard and you demand more from yourself, it will not happen for you. If you want a more fulfilling career, bigger home, more money, better school for your children, or whatever the goal, then you must commit to step up. As long as your wants remain wishes, it is unlikely you'll ever achieve them. Don't be like the person who comes home, eats dinner, watches television, and complains about his circumstances, yet does nothing to change them.

If you are giving all that you have but are miserable at your job and feel you deserve more, then leave. Don't hang around until you're forced out—life is too short. If you feel that you are not being paid what you are worth, then find ways to increase your value within the organization. If you have decided to continue taking a paycheck, then you owe it to yourself and the company you're with to give your best efforts.

I was once told of a builder who had the reputation of being the best builder around. He had worked for years in a large company, and he had reached the age of retirement. Before retiring, his employer asked him to build one more house. The builder accepted this one last job, but his heart was not involved. He used inferior materials and less capable workers. The timber was poor, and he failed to see the many things that should have been clear. When the house was finished, his employer came to him reaching in his pocket and said, "Thank you for all the years you've worked for me. As a gift from me, here is the key. The house is yours. It is a present from me to you." The builder quickly regretted that he had not used the best materials and the most capable workers. If he had only known the house was for him. You and I are the same. The decisions, habits, and life we are creating now is the life we get to live with in the future. In the end, there comes a point when we look back over our lives and determine whether or not we gave it our best. The hope is that you and I can experience what Grandma Moses did when she reached the end of her life and said, "I look back on my life like a good day's work; it is done and I am satisfied with it." If today were your last day to live and you looked over your life, would you be filled with satisfaction and peace, or would you be filled with regret and sadness?

Helen Keller said, "Life is either a daring adventure or nothing." One way to make it a daring adventure is by raising your standards, make new decisions, even take some risks you know in your gut you need to take.

Holding yourself to higher standards is not always easy. You'll find that when you push yourself, mediocre people won't understand. They will, at times, think you're crazy and question why you would work so hard.

Not only was Walt Disney willing to press forward in the face of over three hundred rejections, but he also expected the best out of each creation and would not settle for anything less. While building a tunnel, an engineer suggested, "Walt, it would be cheaper if you built the tunnel straight." Walt replied, "It would be cheaper not to do it at all." It was this standard of excellence that made Disneyland the spectacular success that it is today.

Although Vince Lombardi wasn't the best or most talented player on his team while growing up, he was an example of demanding the best from himself. He once played an entire game after getting a cut in his mouth. Following the game, his cut required thirty stitches. Vince refused to give in and willingly endured the pain until the goal was achieved.

You may be familiar with Roger Bannister, who in 1954 was the first person to break the four-minute mile.

What you may not know is that the man who trained Roger Bannister was Dr. Thomas Kirk Cureton, director of the physical fitness laboratory at the University of Illinois. Dr. Cureton had developed a revolutionary system that could make a person run faster and increase his energy level. The system was based on two principles: 1. Train the whole body. 2. Push yourself to the limit of endurance, extending the limit with each workout. Dr. Cureton said, "The art of record breaking is the ability to take more out of yourself than you've got."

This is the level of commitment and demand one must apply to achieve. If it were anything less, more people would be achieving their dreams. *Almost* isn't enough. In the real world, giving it your almost best is not going to cut it. It will take one hundred percent pure commitment.

Today I make the new commitment to: __________

____

____

____

CHAPTER 4

Taking the Time to Work on You

Law #3

IF YOU WANT MORE, THEN YOU MUST become more. In his classic book *As a Man Thinketh*, James Allen quietly shares a secret that often goes unmentioned. He explains, "Men do not attract that which they *want*, but that which they *are*." Did you catch that?

Whatever you have accumulated into your life, is a reflection of the person you have become. It is a reflection of what you believe is possible, what you truly expect to achieve, the knowledge you have gained, and habits you have formed. If you want more, then you must become more. It will be necessary that you begin taking the time to improve yourself. Remember: "The biggest room in the world is the room for improvement."

Just as you cannot give something you don't have, neither can you achieve something you don't reflect. If you want more money, what type of person must you become in order to make more money? If the marketplace pays you based on the value that you bring to it, what must you do to become more valuable? If you want a better relationship, what must you do to make that a reality? If you want a dream home, a vacation, or any other goal, what must you do to become the person that will attract it?

Even if you successfully get what you want, your new found success may soon disappear if you don't become the person that is equal to or greater than the goal achieved. Think about it. Why is it that new lottery winners lose, squander, or give away their money within a few years of winning it? Why is it that most of them file bankruptcy within five years? The reason is because they have not developed a millionaire mindset. They haven't become the person that is equal to the accomplishment. Therefore, based on the law of attraction, they could not sustain it. Even a mountain climber knows he cannot take short cuts or skip important stages of the climb by simply reaching the summit by helicopter. The climber knows that if he doesn't get properly acclimatized, by ascending gradually, he could become very sick and even die.

Most people are living this principle backward. Instead if living by the philosophy, "Be—Do—Have," they want to "Have—Do—Be." Most people want the interest before they make the investment. They think if they first had a million dollars then they would start doing the things that millionaires do. However, this runs against a law of nature called the law of compensation, which consists of three specific principles. First, is the law of *sowing and reaping*. This means that according to your habits and actions, you attract the results that harmonize with those habits and actions. Therefore, if you are not getting what you want, then change what you are sowing.

When you see a champion break a record, it isn't luck. The difference between first place and second place is usually a fraction of a second. What makes the difference? Perhaps the champion practiced a little harder and a little longer than his opponent? Possibly the champion worked on one bad habit long enough so that he was able to replace it with a more empowering habit. Perhaps this was the slight edge that made the difference.

The second part of the law is the law of *increasing returns*. Not only do you reap what you sow, but you reap *more* than you sow. If you plant a tiny seed in the ground, you reap a huge tree in return. And the third aspect of the law is *delayed gratification*. This means that you reap what you sow *after* you have sowed it. If you planted a seed yesterday, it would be foolish to think you could show up today expecting to reap the harvest. The law of the harvest requires patience once you have invested time and energy.

When you see people achieving their goals, you can be sure they have made the commitment to consistently improve upon their skills and abilities. Before a doctor earns one dollar, she has already invested thousands of dollars and time in herself. The same is true with athletes or musicians. They invest countless hours of practice before the opportunity arises to perform. You must do the same. Benjamin Disraeli said, "The secret of success in life is for a man to be ready for his opportunity when it comes." If a person has not prepared himself sufficiently, when the opportunity comes, it is often too late.

I knew that I wanted to be a speaker. I wanted to use my voice as a tool to inspire and give people tools that could improve the quality of people's lives. I also realized that if I were to capitalize on potential opportunities that would come my way, I had to develop my skills as a speaker.

While in my early twenties, I worked on the staff of a senator in Washington, D. C. At midnight, several times a week, I walked a few blocks down the street to the Marriott Hotel. It was midnight when I would walk upstairs to the ballroom. Making sure no one saw me, I would walk in, close the door behind me, and proceed to the stage that was set up for the convention the next day. There on the stage, with a big marker in my hand—pretending it was a microphone—I would walk back and forth across the stage speaking to the imagined audience that was sitting before me.

At that time in my life, I was reading every book that had anything to do with public speaking. When I watched a speech by someone who impressed me, I would duplicate his movements and body language. I devoted myself to one skill at a time until it became natural. I practiced my stories over and over to be sure I used the right speed, tone, and expressions until I mastered them. When I didn't go to the hotel, I would listen to audiotapes and read books on performance. When my roommates were watching television, they would wonder why I worked so hard. They couldn't understand it and would tell me to just relax. They would suggest that I slow down and smell the roses. Like Garth Brooks, I would think to myself, "I can smell the roses when I'm running with them in my hands." I kept thinking that if I invested in myself now, the dividends would be paid back in multiple rewards.

If you want to be a great salesperson, then make the commitment to learn all you can about the art of selling. Read the books and attend the classes. If you want the results that come from being a better teacher, parent, athlete, or leader, then commit yourself every day to grow and develop in that area. Listen to the audio programs and read the books. Bookstores and libraries are filled with answers. When you are driving in your car, turn off the radio talk shows and listen to something that can really make a difference in your life. Earl Nightingale says, "If a person will spend one hour a day on the same subject for five years, that person will be an expert on that subject." When you think about it, that is an amazing promise.

If you have habits that are preventing you from achieving your goals, then rid yourself of them. If procrastination, laziness, overindulgence, or a bad temper are limiting your effectiveness, then go to work to replace those bad habits with good habits. Psychologist say that ninety percent of our behavior is merely unconsciously based. Once we form habits, we become slaves to them. Therefore, choose your habits wisely.

Improving yourself requires self-discipline. It is not always easy. There will be times when achievement requires you to do things that you don't like to do. Discipline, however, will help you stay on track. It will help you endure to the end without giving into the path of least resistance. Discipline prevents people from engaging in self-indulgent behaviors. People with discipline are in control of themselves and thus have the power to change virtually any aspect of their life.

I suggest that you go from being good to being great in whatever area of personal interest you choose. When you are good, then *good* results are what you will get. And most people are good. Likewise, when you are great, you are more likely to get *great* results. It is a choice! And the only way to become great is to consistently work at it.

Make the commitment to develop your talents. Most people don't develop talents that come easy to them. The easier it is to be good at something the harder it is to be great. Don't let being good stand in the way of being great! Your talents can be your greatest resource—if you develop them. They can also be a great source of inner satisfaction.

No matter how talented you are, growth is not an automatic process. By default, life creates opportunities by which we grow, such as being laid off or changing jobs, struggling with relationships, or raising your children. However, these growth opportunities will not be enough to take you where you want to go. You must make a deliberate effort to grow and change specifically in alignment with your goals.

Part of the process of improving yourself is learning to take advantage of "feedback." When you begin taking action toward achieving your goals or learning a new skill, you will inevitably start getting feedback. Feedback can be both positive and negative, and both can certainly be very useful, even necessary. For example, positive feedback comes from the feeling of satisfaction, receiving awards, compliments, or simply noticing results you are producing. As a result of positive feedback, it usually helps people maintain a high level motivation to continue persevering. Negative feedback, however, may lead some people to question their overall direction. This feedback shows up as pain, disappointment, ridicule, and noticing that you are producing undesirable results.

Feedback, if listened to, will put you "on course" to achieving your goals. Ignored, it will take you "off course" from achieving your goals. *To achieve your goals more rapidly, decide today to welcome, embrace, and learn from all the feedback you receive.* My one last suggestion with feedback is to take into consideration the source. If it is a person, do they have a genuine interest in you achieving your goals? Do they have the credibility to provide feedback on the matter? If not, then be very selective as to what you accept as useful feedback.

Richard Bandler taught, "The mind likes what is the same, but it learns from what is different." If you neglect to learn from the feedback that comes your way, stay in your comfort zone, or continue in your usual, comfortable patterns, then there is no growth or improvement.

Again, some people don't like changing, because

it's easier to stay the same. Some don't change because it leads to uncertainty. Then there are those who don't change, yet expect things to get better around them. You've heard the definition of insanity: "Doing the same thing and expecting a different result." The only way to grow is to be willing to change.

When you reach a plateau or become stagnant, look within yourself before looking to change what's external. All too often, people rush to change their circumstances by changing their spouse, job, or a goal. Your success is more likely to happen if you will instead ask yourself, "What do I need to do to become better in my job? What do I need to do to become more valuable within my organization? What can I do to improve my relationships? What skills and habits do I need to form in place of the bad ones, so that I will be led to better circumstances?" It is far more effective to make internal changes first if you want the external things to change.

Finally, you must make sure that what you learn leads to action. There are many who know much, but neglect to apply their knowledge. Do you know people like that? Someone takes every opportunity to learn and grow. They have soaked up every book, gone to every seminar and may even have multiple college degrees, yet do little with it? The only way knowledge has power is when you apply it.

Once you start applying new skills and knowledge, maintain your momentum. There is nothing more useless than learning new skills that can have a dramatic impact on your achievements and then seldom using them. Like a muscle, when knowledge, skills, and habits go unused, they dissipate. You've heard the phrase "use it or lose it." This is why it is important to make a daily commitment to improve and maintain your good habits once you acquire them. Michael Jordan understood this. He was at the top of his game and undoubtedly the best player in the world. While filming the movie *Space Jam*, he had a basketball court built outside the studio, so that during filming breaks he could maintain his skills. This is a commitment to never-ending improvement. It is an example of holding yourself to high standards, which enabled Jordan to form quality habits; making him one of the best players to ever played the game.

When people continually work on themselves, they become sharper in their thinking. They are equipped with more accurate data that directly corresponds with the quality of decisions they make. They are more likely to come up with effective strategies and solutions. As a result of continually working on themselves, they are more likely to discover what they want and what they are passionate about. Self-improvement leads them not only to achievement, but also to a greater sense of fulfillment.

Not only is it important to take the time to work on yourself, it is equally important to take the time to think. Take time to get away from the daily grind to reflect on what you have learned. Take a little time daily, monthly, and yearly to evaluate and reflect on where you have been, where you are going, and where you want to be.

As you grow, you become more valuable. With your increased value, you are more likely to achieve the goals you set. Whitney Young, Jr. said, "It is better to be prepared for an opportunity and not have one than have an opportunity and not be prepared." To consciously and deliberately spend the time to work on yourself daily is a habit that must be acquired to achieve your goals.

Today I will do the following to improve myself: __

____

____

____

CHAPTER 5

Master Your Thinking

Law #4

IF THERE IS A "GREAT DIVISION" between achievers and non-achievers, it could definitively be tied to the quality of one's thinking. There have been extensive writings on this subject that date back thousands of years. All achievement or defeat is born in the moment of thought. Managing this powerful, yet subtle force, may be your greatest accomplishment in life.

Whatever thoughts you allow to dominate your mind will have a direct impact on what you attract into your life. Like a magnet, each person attracts into his life the people and circumstances that harmonize with his most dominating thoughts. Napoleon Hill made it clear after his classic study of successful people that "thought impulses immediately begin to translate themselves into their physical equivalent, whether those thoughts are voluntary or involuntary."

Emerson said, "We are what we think about all day long." If you allow garbage in, garbage is bound to come out. If you let good thoughts dominate your mind, good is likely to come your way. LIKE ATTRACTS LIKE. If your mind is dominated by thoughts of poverty, you will attract poverty into your life. If your mind is dominated by thoughts of anger, you are more likely to be angry. If you allow thoughts of small achievement to run rampant through your mind, you will achieve the small things in life. The playwright Victor Hugo said, "A small man is made up of small thoughts." On the other hand, if your mind is dominated by your dreams and goals, then you are bound to attract those dreams and goals into your life.

In his classic book, *As a Man Thinketh*, James Allen writes,

> A man does not come to the almshouse or the jail by the tyranny of fate or circumstance, but by the pathway of groveling thoughts and base desires. Nor does a pure-minded man fall suddenly into crime by stress of any mere external force; the criminal thought had

long been secretly fostered in the heart, and the hour of opportunity revealed its gathered power. Circumstance does not make the man; it reveals him to himself.

I love this insight because it underscores the truth of the power of thought. If not managed properly, thoughts can lead to compromise and defeat. They can also lead you to victory.

The same level of thinking that has brought you this far is not going to be enough to take you where you want to go. If I asked: *Who are you? How would you describe yourself? What makes you worthy of your goals? What special attributes or abilities do you process that makes achieving your goals possible?* How would you answer? What are the immediate thoughts that come to your mind? If you want to change your life, begin by changing your thinking. Change the way that you think about yourself, others, and the world. If you have the habit of negative thinking, it will be in your favor to change it and change it now.

Whether out of worry, fear, or habitual affirmations, much of what the average person thinks about is negative. And at the same time we naively wonder why we feel down, discouraged, and aren't achieving our goals the way we would like to. Far too many people have the habit of saying negative phrases to themselves such as, "I can't do that!" "This is the way it's always been." "Things never change!" "I don't have any talents." "I can't find a job." "I have a poor memory." Sometimes we even say demeaning statements, such as "I am such an idiot" or "I'm so stupid."

Just when we are about to commit to a goal, we talk ourselves out of it. We question our ability and even our potential. I can remember when just as I was about to speak to a large audience of teachers, a voice inside me asked, "Who do you think you are? You don't have the same level of education as your audience, and besides you're too young." These thoughts not only made me insecure, they almost convinced me to decline the opportunity to speak.

Unfortunately, many people don't even realize that they are communicating this way. Negative thinking is largely an unconscious process. Thus, often we find it difficult to recognize that we are thinking in such a manner. Therefore, the moment we become aware of self-defeating thoughts pervading our minds, it is vital that we dispel them. More importantly, we must take an active role in discovering these negative thoughts and replace them with useful thoughts.

Negative thoughts are powerful. Maybe you have had the desire to lose weight and you find yourself in the grocery store when this voice creeps up and asks, "Buy yourself a donut." Immediately, you respond, "I don't want to buy a donut. I am trying to lose weight." You would think the voice would go away, but it is persistent. The voice comes back and says, "Come on, you deserve it. You've been eating great the last few days. You can afford to treat yourself." So you decide to buy the donut and you think, "One little bite won't hurt." And before you know it that one little bite turns into a second and third bite and quickly the donut is gone. Then you think, "Well, since I've ruined my diet for today, another donut won't hurt. I'll start over tomorrow." Can you relate to this?

You can't stop yourself from thinking nor can you always control what thoughts enter your mind, but you can control what you focus and dwell upon. W. Clement Stone said, "The power of thought is the only thing over which any human being has complete unquestionable means of control."

When a negative thought or pattern of thinking enters your mind, don't speak it; set it aside, forget about it, or replace it. When such a thought occurs to you, immediately stop and say to yourself, "Erase." "What I mean is . . ." Then begin to focus on something positive about the situation. This is not to say that negative things don't happen. They do, but it is more effective to be solution-focused than obstacle-focused. The goal is to prevent yourself from holding on to and replaying negative thoughts.

If you saw a movie you didn't like, would you go back to see it again? Let alone over and over? Of course not! Yet, many people do this inside their minds. They make a mistake or encounter a failure and they play the worst aspect of that experience over and over inside their minds. Remember, you are the creator of your life and whatever thoughts you consistently sow you will also reap. When you find yourself experiencing negative thoughts, stop and change the picture to a more positive one. Change what you focus on in relationship to that experience. Choose a new angle. Begin focusing on the benefits of the experience, rather than the pain. Think about it. If you are going to think something over and over, you might as well make it good.

Thoughts are the cause, and the conditions they create are the effect. In other words, all the conditions or experiences we encounter in our lives are created by our thoughts. Many of our outward expressions are the result of our internal feelings, which are caused by our thoughts. If you think angry thoughts, it will become easier to be angry. If your mind is occupied with thoughts of depression, you are likely to feel depressed. Likewise, if you fill your mind with positive, pleasant thoughts, you will attract positive and pleasant experiences. Your thoughts also have the tendency to reveal themselves in your facial expressions and even in your overall countenance. They are literally reflected by the way a person carries himself.

If you feel emotional pain in your life from a past failure, defeat, broken relationship, or loss of some kind, it is the result of your thinking, not the circumstance itself. In his book *Your Erroneous Zones*, Wayne Dyer said, "If you are experiencing an inner discontent as a result of what someone said or did, what you are really saying in that moment is . . . 'What that person thinks of me is more important than what I think of myself.'" What people say can affect what we think of ourselves. If we don't stand up within, the opinions of others can spread like wildfire burning down anything in its path.

The most powerful product of thoughts are the beliefs they form. Once we believe something is true, we begin gathering evidence to support that belief. We then unconsciously make those beliefs our personal truth and reality.

Whatever you repeat consistently, you will begin to believe. Once you believe, you either open yourself up for the possibilities that stand before you, or you close yourself off from them. If you think you're ugly, worthless, and stupid, you may begin to believe it. Likewise, if you think of yourself as beautiful, worthy, and smart, you will eventually believe that, too, and begin behaving accordingly.

If you have the habit of saying the phrase, "I can't," then give up the phrase. Go from saying, "I can't. . ." to adding one word, "I can't. . . *yet.*" to ultimately saying, "I CAN!" This ugly four letter word, "can't," is extremely powerful in that it is very negative. If not eliminated, it has the potential to control your life.

I can still remember the day I eliminated the "I can't" phrase from my vocabulary and I owe a lot of gratitude to a high school senior who taught me a very important lesson. I can remember in the eighth grade going to the high school to participate in sports. One of the sports I chose was track and field, in which I pole-vaulted. On the team was a state champion pole-vaulter who I looked up to. He was popular and always respectful. I never saw him get upset, nor did he ever put anyone down. In many ways I wanted to be like him. Then one day, as I was learning how to pole vault, when struggling to make it over a relatively low bar, I became frustrated. All of my other teammates seemed to do it effortlessly. After a dozen or more attempts I became so frustrated that I defiantly threw my pole down on the ground and angrily said, "I can't do it!" I was about to learn a lesson that has impacted every aspect of my life. Immediately upon saying, "I can't do it!" this state champion pole-vaulter calmly walked over to me, looked me directly in the eyes and said, "Can't, never could do it! " I was taken aback, humbled, and openly receptive. In that moment he taught me a very important lesson. A lesson I shall never forget. He encouraged me in that split moment to give up the "I can't..." phrases, because "Can't never could..."

Using the word "can't, " or any other negative phrase, systematically shuts off any possibility to succeed. Simply put, our self-talk creates and controls our self-images, beliefs, and comfort zones. As a result, those self-images, beliefs, and comfort zones determine our performance. Thus, our low performance cycles around, confirming and stimulating our self-talk. It is a endless loop of reinforcing behavior. Unless we take control of our thinking, we cannot improve our performance. By continually talking or thinking about our present circumstances as they are, we are reinforcing the likelihood of remaining where we are. Albert Einstein said, "The significant problems we face cannot be solved by the same level of thinking that created them." We must change our thinking. Our current level of thinking that has brought us this far in life will not be enough to help us get where we want to go. We must change our thinking from focusing on where we are, to focusing on the future we want to achieve as though we already achieved it. Making this important shift in our thinking will be discussed in chapter

7, *Operating from Your Imagination.*

Some people are in habit of asking lousy questions. They ask, "Why do I always screw up?" "Why don't things ever work out for me?" We fall in the trap of asking these lousy questions and guess what happens? Our mind does exactly what it is designed to do, which is to come up with answers. As a result of lousy questions, we get a lousy answers. You've heard the phrase, "Ask and ye shall receive." Has it ever dawned on you that by simply changing the questions you ask yourself, you can change your thinking and thereby the results you attract in to your life? For example, you could change "Why do I always screw up?" to "What must I do better next time? Or change from, "Why don't things ever work out for me?" to "What must I do differently to ensure succeeding at this task in the future?"

Your thoughts can either create fear, or they can create confidence. They can create pain, or they can create resolve and joy. Your thoughts can lead you to take action or they can drive you to withdraw and even give up. Likewise, Virgil said, "They can because they think they can."

How do you control your thoughts? Make certain that whatever you allow into your mind is healthy and positive. It is vital that you begin today by engaging in uplifting conversations with yourself and others. Be wise with your television and news intake. Be aware of the books and magazines that you read. Do they uplift you? Do they inspire you to stretch and grow for the better? Or, do they gossip and speak ill of others? Each one of these activities, if not cautiously managed, can dramatically affect you. You may not see signs of their existence today or tomorrow, but sooner or later they will begin affecting your behavior and performance.

Although you may be filling your mind with uplifting material, destructive thoughts still have a way of surfacing. A simple strategy I have found to reduce the impact of such thoughts is to immediately change your physiology once you become aware of the negative thought. When speaking of physiology I am referring to the way a person uses or carries his physical body. From the way that you stand, sit, use your facial expressions, and more all play a significant role in what you experience internally. If a self-defeating thought enters your mind, stand up, take a walk, or simply engage in an activity that will distract you from dwelling on the thought. This immediately disrupts the pattern of negative thinking and helps prevent the thought from taking root.

Therefore, get in the habit of changing your physiology to support the desired positive thought that you plan to focus on. Your physiology plays a central role in the quality of your thinking. When you put your body in a position that reflects a confident and calm person, thoughts have the tendency of internally experiencing the feelings of confidence and calmness. Use this strategy to redirect and refocus your thoughts.

Distracting yourself may be effective for the moment, but will not always serve long-term. Therefore, another useful strategy is to get in the habit of recognizing destructive thinking when it arises and stop it immediately. In a disciplined way, cut off its nourishment. If negative or self-defeating thoughts persist, then evaluate their accuracy. Start looking for evidence that will make the negative thought inaccurate. Often our negative thoughts are groundless and unsupported in reality.

Once you have moved your body and begun focusing on something new, look at your goals and say to yourself—*It's possible!* You must not only think in terms of general possibility, but also begin thinking it is possible for you personally. Begin seeing yourself achieving what you want and allow that picture to dominate your mind.

Get in the habit of standing up inside yourself every day and convincing yourself that you have what it takes. Every day you must convince yourself that you are unstoppable. Convince yourself every day that your goals have value. It is vital that what you think and say to yourself reflects your expectation that your goals can and will be accomplished. These are the dominating thoughts you want occupying your mind.

Lastly, goals give direction to the mind. When you are living with purpose, you don't have the time or desire to waste energy engaging in negative thinking. Your mind is occupied with achieving your goals.

As you alter your thoughts toward people, they will in turn alter their thoughts toward you. If you alter your thoughts about your world, your world will change to be consistent with those thoughts. If you will alter your thoughts away from those things you fear, the fear will dissipate. There is an African proverb that states, "If there is no enemy within, the enemy on the outside can do us no harm." If you alter the way you think about yourself, this will alter what you attract into your day-to-day experience.

Any seed nourished will eventually bear fruit, good or bad. What fruit are you yielding? What are you thinking? Whatever you think about consistently, you will eventually attract. Think wisely!

What are the random negative thoughts or beliefs I will begin to control or eliminate? ________________

____

____

What are the positive thoughts I will replace them

with? ______________________________________

CHAPTER 6

What Do You Want?

Law #5

FIVE YEARS FROM NOW YOU ARE going to arrive. The question is where? If you don't know what you want, how will you ever recognize it when you have it? The truth is, if you don't know what you want, you are likely to wind up getting nowhere very quickly. Without direction, it's just a matter of time before you are working at a job or staying in a relationship that you dislike, or living a life that is unfulfilling.

Unfortunately, most people are what Zig Ziglar calls "wandering generalities." These are people who wander through life without direction. They are not reaching for worthwhile goals. They mingle through life like spectators, watching the game on the field. Ziglar says, "If you were to ask a climber how he climbed the tallest mountain, I doubt he would say, 'Well—I just started wandering around and ended up here.'"

Achievers know *exactly what they want and consistently move toward it.* It is amazing how many people don't know what they want in life. Among the many people I have worked with, I am amazed at how many people go from one day to the next not knowing where they really intend to go or a vague idea of what they would like their future to become.

I mentioned earlier that you attract based on the sum total of your dominating thoughts. Once you are clear about what you want, the universe works day and night to help attract it into your life. Opportunities will show up out of nowhere. You'll begin recognizing things that you otherwise would have never noticed before. In many cases, you will realize that these opportunities were right in front of you the whole time.

Maxwell Maltz described this power as a servo-mechanism, "an automatic goal-seeking machine which 'steers' its way to a target or a goal by use of feedback data and stored information automatically correcting course when necessary." Our mind has a way of focussing on what we want and filtering out information that is not important to us—it is a survival mechanism.

If you were unable to filter all the data that is constantly bombarding your brain, you would go crazy. For example, place this book down for a moment and do the following exercise. Become still and notice all the sounds that are present, that a moment ago you weren't even aware. Maybe you hear the air-conditioning, people shifting or walking around. Maybe you notice your breathing or cars driving outside your home or office. You have a built-in system that tunes out what is not important to you.

The bottom line is, if you are unclear about what you want out of life, then even if opportunities arise, they will simply go unnoticed. You will unknowingly filter them out. On the other hand, when you are clear about what you want to achieve, you will notice the slightest opportunity that can lead to the accomplishment of your goal.

This is called the law of attraction—a combination of knowing what you want and directing your thoughts accordingly. When I worked with Tony Robbins, it wasn't an accident. When I wrote my first script for a motion picture, or helped build a multi million-dollar company, it wasn't an accident. When I look at all the opportunities that have revealed themselves to me over the years, I am convinced that they came as a result of clearly knowing what I wanted and living my life in such a way that made those goals attainable.

For years I've wanted to write a book. Then one night I was listening to an audiotape of Charles "Tremendous" Jones. While listening, I noticed a phone number on the cassette tape label. The set of tapes must have been thirty years old and most people wouldn't have given the number another thought. However, I did. I thought to myself, "I wonder if this phone number is still active?" It was eleven o'clock at night and I dialed the phone number and it began ringing. Then, just as I was about to hang up, someone answered. The voice on the other end said, "Who is this?"

In response, I said, "Who is this?" After a short pause I got the feeling I'd better tell him, so I gave him my name.

I then asked, "May I ask with whom am I speaking?"

I can still remember him saying in a low voice, "This is Charles 'Tremendous' Jones."

Surprised I said, "You've got to be kidding me! This is *the* Charles 'Tremendous' Jones?"

He said, "That's me!"

I asked, "Where do you live?"

He said, "Pennsylvania."

I quickly apologized. "Please tell me I didn't wake

you up."

"Oh, no," he replied.

I said, "It is one o'clock in the morning," and I inquired why he was up at that hour. He proceeded to tell me he was reading a book.

I remember visiting with him for probably forty minutes or so as he shared some advice about writing a book. Toward the end of our discussion he asked me for my fax number, which I gave him. When I woke the next morning I had a twenty-page fax sent to me with more advice. On the cover page was a handwritten note that I still cherish today.

Among other things, "I'm looking forward to reading your manuscript," read the note. This experience was not simply a coincidence!

Eight months later I was reading a book called *The Joy of Failure* by Wayne Allyn Root. It was a Saturday morning about 9:00 a.m. when I completed the book and noticed a phone number on the last page. Would it surprise you if I told you that I dialed the number? Would it surprise you if I said that Mr. Root answered the phone? Well, that is exactly what happened. That morning he was in his office all alone when he answered the phone. We talked for about ten minutes, and he shared his strategy for writing a book.

He said, "If you will write an hour and a half each

day, by the end of a year you will have written a two-hundred-page book." Coincidence? No!

Eight months later I was in Southern California when I was reminded that the renowned author and trainer Brian Tracy's office was near where I was staying. After downloading the directions from the Internet, I drove to his office. He travels frequently, so I knew it was unlikely that he would be there, but I wanted to tour of his office. When I arrived, the secretary was puzzled by my request. She said she had never been asked to give a tour before, and that she would need to speak to her supervisor. When she stood up to leave, I asked her if Brian Tracy ever came in the office.

She said, "Normally, no."

The word "normally" came off her lips a little hesitantly, so I inquired about her use of the word.

She responded, "Typically, when Mr. Tracy comes into town from being on the road, he works out of his home in an effort to spend as much time as possible with his family."

However, she did say that he happened to be in the office that particular morning. Upon hearing that information, I immediately asked if I could meet Mr. Tracy, too. She said that she wasn't sure and left to ask her supervisor.

Let me stop right here and say that when you are

clear about what you want, it is important to impress the mind with as much detail as possible. It is important to create a very clear picture of what you want. I thought by having a tour of his office it might provide supportive detail. I wanted to see what "my future office" might look like. The secretary left the foyer, and two minutes later the president walked up and asked how he could help me. I explained that I wanted a tour of the office and explained why.

I continued, "Since Mr. Tracy is in the office I'd like to meet him, too." He told me he would see what he could do.

Two minutes later I remember looking down the office hallway from the foyer watching Brian Tracy walk right toward me. I'll never forget the sight. Six-feet tall, white hair, wearing jeans, flip-flops, Hawaiian shirt, and a big smile.

He walked right up to me with his hand out to shake mine and said, "Hi, I'm Brian Tracy."

I said, "Hi, I'm TJ Hoisington."

We visited for a few minutes, and he proceeded to give me a tour of his office. Once we made it back to the foyer, and just as our visit came to a close, I remembered the words of a speaker who said, "Always act when the emotion is high."

I told Mr. Tracy that I recently started writing a

book and asked if he would be willing to read the manuscript and write an endorsement.

He thought for a moment and said, "I'd be happy to. Send me the first chapter and the table of contents . . ."

Not only did Brian Tracy endorse this book, but also Wayne Allyn Root and Charles "Tremendous" Jones lent their support. Not only was I committed to working on myself, but also I was committed to my goal.

Again, were these experiences simply coincidence or luck? Definitely not. In fact, the story doesn't even stop there. A few months later I happened to be at the right place at the right time and met Jack Canfield, co-author of the best-selling book *Chicken Soup for the Soul.* Not only did Jack endorse this book, he spent time giving me five pointers that could make my book a success.

These experiences were neither coincidence nor were they luck. (Branch Rickey, the Brooklyn Dodgers', general manager often remarked, "Luck is the residue of design.") They were the result of a clear vision and commitment to achieving what I wanted. My clear goals influenced my thoughts and decisions that enabled me to gravitate toward opportunities that supported my desires. The same can happen for you.

What is even more amazing is that initially you don't need to know *how* you are going to reach your goal.

I found that if you will first become clear about what you want and why you want it, then *how* to achieve it will reveal itself at the appropriate time. Your reasons come first and answers come second. Once you are clear and committed about what you want, the law of attraction is set in motion.

Am I saying that having a strategy is not important? Of course not! There is a time when having a strategy and plan is vitally important, but initially it is more important to know *what* you want, *why* you want it, and then make a commitment that you are going to achieve it. Many people spend so much energy worrying about "how" to do something that it becomes overwhelming and they decide not to go after the goal at all. Some people suffer from "analysis-paralysis," a condition in which people analyze profusely, yet *do* nothing. The law dictates that once you decide *what* you want and *why* you want something, the "how" will make itself known at the appropriate time.

Another important aspect of knowing what you want is: Be sure you dwell on what you want rather than dwelling on what you don't want. I'll often ask people what they want out of life or out of an experience, and they immediately begin explaining what they *don't* want or what they want to avoid. They focus on the fear or the disappointment of failure, rather than focusing on the reward of taking the risk. Whatever image you hold in your mind will begin to reflect itself in your world.

It is also important to be specific. To say you want a nice house is not enough to start attracting a nice house. Instead, make the picture so vivid that you can describe the style and color of the house. Describe the size and any unique characteristics of the house. What about the yard or driveway? Is price important to you? This much detail is necessary. If more money is important, then how much will do? How much will that amount divide out to each month, week, or day? What will it look like to achieve the goal? And most importantly, why is it important to you? What are all the benefits? And then write each answer down on paper. This level of clarity will enable you to effectively hone in on your dreams.

The most important part of getting what you want is to begin dreaming about it. Dreaming creates a burning desire that turns possibility into reality. Imagine if money, time, talent, and education were not obstacles. What would you go after? What are you passionate about? What would keep you up late at night and get you up early in the morning. George Burns once said, "I would rather fail at something that I love than succeed at something I hate." It is vital that you take time out—spend time in solitude if needed—and decide what you would love to do above all else. What inspires you? Reflect on what interests you have. What comes easily to you and simultaneously gives you a sense of satisfaction? These answers should serve as clues to discovering what you want.

Think big by making a list of 20 things you would love to do. Then think of ways you can design your life around those 20 things. If you find it somewhat difficult to come up with what you want, begin asking yourself the question, "If I did know, what would it be?" Ask this over and over and your brain will eventually start giving you the answers. Then write these thoughts down on a piece of paper. Keep in mind that whatever you like doing there is a way to make a living at it.

If you find yourself at the point where you think you know what you want, yet not really sure, I suggest that you take some small action toward that desired goal. This allows you to get a "taste" of the particular goal. If the "taste" is satisfactory and you get the impression this is something that may work for you—be decisive and go for it!

There is no such thing as an unrealistic goal. Your time frame, *current* condition, or strategy may be ineffective or unrealistic, like a three-hundred-pound jockey and expecting to win the race. Or entering the ring to box Muhammad Ali—some things are ridiculously insane. But for the most part, the goals you choose will be attainable. Granted, your goals may require that you stretch, grow, and improve. Some goals will require that you develop new skills. Others will require that you change your environment. Whatever it is, there are some things out of your control, but there are many things that are within your control. All too often people kill a goal before they ever have a chance of letting it take shape because they believe it is too far out of our reach. However, I like the advice Price Pritchett once gave, "If you are going to doubt something, doubt your limits."

Mortimer Adler said, "If you don't strive for the high things in life, you'll settle for the low." My good friend Bob Moawad says, "Most people don't aim too high and miss, they aim too low and hit." Remember, the size of your goals determines the size of your results—so dream BIG. Dream bigger than you ever thought you could dream! Big dreams attract big people. Big dreams attract big opportunities. Big dreams create big results.

When you mix vision with commitment, unforeseen things will happen that will help turn your goals into reality. Goethe writes,

> Until one is committed there is hesitancy, the chance to draw back, always ineffectiveness. Concerning all acts of initiative, there is one elementary truth, the ignorance of which kills countless ideas and splendid plans: that the moment one definitely commits oneself, then Providence moves too. All sorts of things occur to help one that would never otherwise have occurred. A whole stream of events, issues from the decision, raising

> in one's favor all manner of unforeseen incidents and meetings and material assistance, which no man could have dreamt would come his way. Whatever you can do, or you can dream, begin it. Boldness has genius, power, and magic in it.

Never let it be said of you that you didn't know what you wanted. Never let it be said that you lived other people's dreams and goals. Decide *today* that you will become clear about what you want and make a commitment to achieve it.

I am passionate and committed about what? If money, time, resource, or opportunity were not an obstacle—what would I *choose* to do? ________________

____

____

CHAPTER 7

Operating from Your Imagination

Law #6

YOUR IMAGINATION IS A MAJOR SOURCE of desire and motivation. It is the primary source to creating change and it is the incubator of all ideas that eventually make their way into reality. Before any song is ever sung, building ever erected, invention ever created, or change ever made, it is first breathed into life in someone's imagination. In the *Laws of Success*, Napoleon Hill taught, "All achievement starts in the imagination before it is ever realized in the physical form."

Achievers get what they want because they utilize the power of their imagination in a very resourceful way.

It is the imagination that takes the invisible and makes it visible.

This was the case of Fred Smith, who gave birth to the idea of the overnight shipping business now known as FedEx. Using his imagination, Walt Disney created an empire in such a way that no one had done before. Conrad Hilton of Hilton Hotels imagined himself owning a hotel long before he ever bought one. The same is true with people like Bill Gates, who created Microsoft, or Ray Kroc, who through McDonalds, created the model for fast food restaurants. They and thousands of others all started with an idea and used their imaginations to turn these ideas into reality.

Often, these individuals didn't have special education or knowledge. They used their imaginations in such ways that they made new combinations with the knowledge they already possessed. Look at Baskin and Robbins, two brothers who had a dream of starting a business. What was their successful idea? They simply opened a shop serving ice cream with thirty-one different flavors. Baskin-Robbins' success wasn't the result of a vast knowledge base or being privy to some think-tank collection of cutting-edge ideas. Rather, they simply used their imaginations in a creative way.

The entire South was changed by the power of one man's use of his imagination. While watching his cat trying to claw a chicken through the walls of its coop, Eli Whitney noticed that the cat was only successful at getting a paw full of feathers. Thus, an idea was born. He imagined an iron claw pulling cotton from a cotton plant. As a result, Eli invented a revolutionary machine: the cotton gin. Again, the power of the imagination.

After a meeting with the founder of Polaroid Corporation, Steve Jobs, the founder of Apple Computer and the music Ipod said, "It's like when I walk in a room, and I want to talk about a product that hasn't even been invented yet. I can see the product as if it is sitting there, right in the center of the table. What I've got to do is materialize it and bring it to life." Unbelievable!

Most people are living by the belief "I'll believe it when I see it." On the other hand, achievers understand "When they believe it, then they'll see it." They understand that, if they can imagine it, it is likely they can achieve it. Outlandish or not, if you can "see" it, then believe in it and begin finding reasons and means that will turn the thought into reality.

Such was the case with actor Jim Carrey before he ever made it to the big screen. Carrey believed in his dream so much that "as a gesture of faith, he wrote himself a check for ten million dollars for 'acting services rendered' and carried it in his wallet for seven years." As a result of his imagination and his belief in his internal picture, he literally began to structure his life around that desire. Operating from his imagination enabled him to "see" what he wanted to have happen in his mind's eye as though he had already achieved it.

Jim Carrey himself said:

> I've always believed in magic. When I wasn't doing anything in this town, I'd go up every night, sit on Mulholland Drive, look out at the city, stretch out my arms, and say, "Everybody wants to work with me. I'm a really good actor. I have all kinds of great movie offers." I'd just repeat these things over and over, literally convincing myself that I had a couple of movies line up. I'd drive down that hill, ready to take the world on, going, "Movie offers are out there for me, I just don't hear them yet." It was like total affirmations, antidotes to the stuff that stems from my family background.

Consciously operating from your imagination is a necessary habit to acquire. Begin thinking in terms of "fake it until you make it" or "acting as if" you have already achieved your goals. Charles F. Kettering, inventor with over 140 patents and honorary doctorates from nearly 30 universities said, "Believe and *act as if* it were impossible to fail." Make your goals as internally vivid as possible. What does it look like? What does it feel like? How did you achieve it—as if you already had? What steps did you take that led to success?

In his book *Golf My Way*, Jack Nicklaus writes, "First I see the ball where I want it to finish, nice and white and sitting up there on the bright green grass. Then, I see the scene quickly change and I see the ball going there, its path, trajectory, and shape, even its behavior on the landing. Then there is sort of a fade out and the next scene shows me making the kind of swing that will turn the previous images into reality." Jack started with the end in mind, as though he already accomplished his desired result.

Unfortunately, most people perform based on memories of their past performances, thus allowing their past performances, good or bad, to govern future performances. They think in terms of "I've never done it before, what makes me think I can do it now?" Because of this type of thinking, if unsuccessful past attempts are dominating our minds, then we will perform accordingly.

However, people who achieve greatness have made a definite habit of operating from their imagination. They understand they cannot drive forward through life while looking through the rearview mirror.

Imagine playing golf and never scoring below ninety. Then imagine taking a seven-year break, and the next time you played you shot a seventy-four. I'm sure you would agree that would be remarkable. Well, that is exactly what happened to Major Nesmeth. Years ago he was sent to Vietnam during the Vietnam War and was eventually captured. He then spent the next seven years in a small cage that was only four feet by four feet in and only four and a half feet tall. To prevent himself from going insane he spent his waking moments imagining himself playing golf. Seven days a week he imagined everything from the clothes he wore, to his grip and swing. He imagined the ball flying through the air and landing precisely where he wanted it to land. Day after day he played the perfect game inside his mind's eye, while in reality he was restricted and suffering. By the time he was released from prison seven years later, his imagined game had become such a part of him that rather than picking up where he had left off, he dramatically improved his game—by nothing more than his imagination.

Had he repeatedly imagined his *past* performance of never scoring below ninety during those seven years, his game would have remained the same. Instead, he imagined a better game, and conditioned it into his mind, which allowed his physical performance to harmonize with his internal picture.

Before I ever gave my first speech, I rehearsed it hundreds of times in my mind's eye. I then relied heavily on the successful image I had created. Although I inevitably made mistakes, I kept my focus on the successful performances and then adjusted accordingly. Eventually, through mentally reviewing the internal picture that I held for myself, I became exactly who I am today. The same will work in your life. If there is an area in your life that you would like to improve, then begin imagining your behavior as though you have already improved in that area. What does it look like? What does it feel like? How do others perceive you? Imagine it as vividly as possible and it will start to affect your performance. Harvard University researchers found that those students who visualized in advance, performed tasks with almost 100% accuracy. Students who did not visualize performing their tasks in advance, achieved only 55% accuracy.

A powerful, yet widely accepted truth about the mind is that it cannot always tell the difference between something that is vividly imagined and that which actually happens. Some psychologists claim that seven hours of visualization is equal to one hour of actual experience. Other psychologists suggest that visualizing accompanied with emotion is sixty times as powerful as a real event. Have you ever had the experience of lying in bed and being frightened by an object in the room, only to turn on the lights or wake up the next morning to find that it was only a familiar object out of place? Although in reality the cause of your fear was inaccurate, it sure felt real, didn't it?

Imagine taking a lemon and cutting it into two pieces. You pick up one half of the lemon, position it over your mouth and squeeze it until lemon juice falls onto your tongue. If you imagine this vividly enough you will have felt some physical sensation. The cause of the sensation had little to do with reality, yet it still had a sensory impact.

Have you ever been driving down the road when the thought of a past experience popped into your mind that made you feel embarrassed, fearful, or even depressed? We have already talked about thoughts and the same is true with the pictures you play in your imagination—they become true to you. We must be careful what we allow to take shape inside our minds. Anything that is continually repeated or imagined will eventually be accepted as your personal truth and reality.

How does this apply to you? If you can't see yourself earning more money, you probably won't. The same is true with owning your own business or taking a risk. If you can't see yourself creating the result you desire, it is unlikely you will make progress in that area. If you can't picture yourself performing or behaving to the best of your ability, it is unlikely you'll make that a reality.

If you picture and say, "I can't," "I feel depressed," "I'll never be able to afford that," "I'm ugly," then your mind will take you at your word. Learning to operate from your imagination is one of the strongest tools you have to produce the results you want.

For just a moment, allow me to be a little technical.

There are two primary purposes of the subconscious mind. The first is to store everything. It stores everything you have ever seen, heard, smelt, and felt with emotion. It stores all your life experiences, knowledge, skills, self-images, even your personality. This data is stored in the subconscious mind as your "truth and reality." The second purpose of the subconscious mind is to "make you act like you." Its purpose is to keep you in harmony with the information it has gathered and stored over the years. In other words, the subconscious mind compels you to act and behave in alignment with your dominate "reality."

Joseph Murphy in his book *The Power of the Subconscious Mind* uses the analogy of the captain and the engine of the ship to illustrate the differing roles of the conscious and subconscious minds. He explains that the captain of the ship is like unto the conscious mind. The captain is the master of the ship, he is in charge. He controls all the instruments, gauges, boilers, and the crew in the engine room. Ultimately, the captain controls the direction of the ship. Below the deck is the engine room; this represents the subconscious mind. It is the source of power, the very power that moves the ship from one location to the other. He explains that if the captain on the bridge of the ship decided to send orders to the engine room to turn the ship onto the rocks, the crew would simply follow his orders. The crew in the engine room cannot see where the captain is leading them. They just know that he is in charge. The engine doesn't talk back. It simply carries out whatever the captain commands. The subconscious mind works in the same fashion. It takes whatever information is given it by the conscious mind, and goes to work to make it reality.

How does this affect you? Simply, whatever phrases you repeatedly speak or pictures you imagine, will eventually be imprinted in your subconscious mind and be accepted as "truth and reality." Once the information has been received, it is the job of the subconscious mind to make you act like you; meaning it causes you to act, behave, and perform in harmony with your dominate thoughts and beliefs. In other words, if you continue to say phrases such as, "I can't" or "I always screw up" or "I'll never get a good job" or "I'll never earn more than $30,000," the subconscious will see to it that the task "can't" be done or that you will not be in a position to get the good job or increase your income.

Henry Ford must have known what he was talking about when he said, "Whether you think you can or think you can't, you are right." Why? Once we form a belief, we immediately start gathering evidence to support the belief, whether it is positive or negative. Therefore, begin consciously creating the pictures you *want* to become your future reality. This is also one way to stretch your comfort zone; by bombarding your subconscious mind with new thoughts and images that reflect what you *want*, rather than what you *don't want*.

Take a few minutes every day to imagine and be creative. Practice this principle. It may not come naturally, but with practice your ability will increase. Ralph Waldo Emerson said, "That which we persist in doing becomes easier—not that the nature of the task has changed, but our ability to do it has increased."

When you fear something and yet desire to feel calm and collected, simply change your fearful internal picture to a calm and centered picture in spite of your circumstances. Are you focusing too heavily on your past, or are you anticipating failure in the future? Change your internal channel and refocus your thoughts.

Because the pictures we imagine are the primary cause of fear, here is a simple strategy you can use to overcome fear: Allow yourself for a moment to imagine the scenario that is creating the fear. Then switch the picture and see yourself in that same scenario performing successfully. Repeat this newly constructed picture as many times as needed, until it is conditioned. While rehearsing this successful picture from beginning to end as vividly as possible, simultaneously say to yourself those phrases and statements that you would say if you were truly confident and able. "Good things happen to me." "I'm excited and ready." "I'm unstoppable!" and "I can do it!"

By imagining a successful outcome, you not only reduce the negative emotions associated with taking action, but you can also eliminate them. Allow yourself to feel elated by your imagined successful performance as you play it over and over. In fact, play the successful performance over and over a minimum of ten times to condition it into your mind. Then, once in a resourceful and confident state of mind, be sure to act. Taking action in that moment will greatly contribute to conquering your fear.

You can even use your imagination to change a behavior. If there are triggers in your environment that lead you to anger, depression, or discouragement, then use your imagination to overcome them.

If you have the habit of getting angry when walking through the front door into a mess, use your imagination to picture yourself being calm, collected, and even happy in spite of the mess. Then when you walk through the door, you will be more likely to behave accordingly. You can even imagine yourself walking through the front door, and going over to your spouse fast enough to give him or her a hug before you have time to notice the mess. Once you have done this, be sure to follow through according to that image. Following through will impress the image deeper into the mind and begin the process of making it a real habit.

Whether you are learning a new skill, changing an area of your life, or working on a specific goal, it is necessary to rehearse and experience what you want to have happen ahead of time. Brian Tracy said, "Winners make a habit of manufacturing their own positive expectations in advance of the event, expecting the very best to come out of their efforts, even though they have no information on which to base it."

Dreams are formed in the imagination and since "life is but a dream" dream on.

Today I will begin operating from my imagination to improve in this specific area of my performance: ______

____

____

____

CHAPTER 8

Action: The Winner's Edge

Law #7

WHAT IS THE MAJOR DIFFERENCE BETWEEN the successful and the unsuccessful? Albert E. N. Gray said, "The common denominator is that the successful were willing to *do* the things that the unsuccessful people were not willing to do." Action is what separates wishful thinkers from those who turn their ideas and goals into reality. You can have all the inspiration, knowledge, and even talent in the world, but if you don't take action, nothing will happen.

Inspiration must lead to action. Operating from your imagination goes beyond dreaming and wishful thinking—

it leads the committed person to take the necessary action that will turn the internal picture into reality. Being clear about your purpose and goals will put you in the top 5% of high achievers. In order to reach the top 1% all you have to do is decide on specific action steps and then begin taking action.

Recently, I had an idea for a movie script. While watching a movie with my family I realized that a sequel to this popular movie had never been written or produced. Somehow it slipped under the Hollywood radar. I couldn't get the idea out of my head. Even though, I had never thought of myself as a screenwriter, I thought—why not! I've always believed in possibilities. Did I ever have doubts? Yes—of course. There were times when that negative voice would enter my thinking and try to convince me I was incapable. But the idea was clear and after debating within, I *decided* to go for it. I was going to live the principles I teach, even if the goal seemed to be a far reach. One night, unable to sleep, I got out of bed at 1 o'clock in the morning and started typing an outline for the story. I typed throughout the night. The next day I continued thinking about it. So I called some friends together and told them about my idea. They all thought the story was great and that it definitely had potential, but they proceeded to remind me that none of us had ever written a movie script before. They said, "We don't know where to start." "We don't have any contacts." "There must me an easier way."

After they left that night, I was reminded that there were many people before the Wright brothers that had envisioned flying, yet they did little about it. Many people before Alexander Graham Bell thought about the concept of the telephone, yet no one ever successfully turned the idea into reality. Others had thoughts and ambitions about cars before Henry Ford began massively producing them. What made them different? What separated the achievers from the thousands of unachievers? The answer is quite simple—action.

Have you ever had an idea for something that you knew people would like, and then walked into a store and noticed it on the shelf? What was the difference between you and that other person? The difference was, that person took action on his idea.

Time and time again I read about people who didn't wait around for opportunities to simply show up. Instead, when all else failed, they created them. In the 1970s, Sylvester Stallone was financially broke after writing several scripts that were all rejected. But he didn't give up; he didn't resign himself to the bleak outlook that his goals as a writer and actor were not possible. Instead he continued taking action and looking for his break. Then one night in 1975 he found himself inspired by watching a boxing match between Chuck Wepner and Muhammad Ali. Although the odds were greatly against Wepner, thirty-to-one, he surprisingly withstood fifteen beating rounds, before being defeated by the great Muhammad Ali. Returning home, Stallone immediately began writing the script that would not only change his life, but became the mega-hit movie *Rocky*. Written in three days, created on a budget of one million dollars, and filmed in twenty-eight days, *Rocky* is one of the biggest successes in the film industry, grossing over $100 million.

Nia Vardalos was another person who was tired of casting agents telling her "Next!" So she created a one-woman play that eventually led to the successful movie *My Big Fat Greek Wedding*. True achievers make it a habit of not sitting around waiting for their break; they create it. They take action! Howard Schultz, Starbucks Coffee's founder and chairman asks, "What distinguishes the talented person who makes it from the person who has even more talent but doesn't get ahead? Part of what constitutes success is timing and chance. But most of us have to create our own opportunities and be prepared to jump when we see the big one others can't see."

In my case, I had never written a movie script before. I didn't know the format or rules for properly writing one, but I did believe it was *possible*. I was also willing to take necessary action. I thought to myself, either

I am going to write the script or sooner or later someone else will. So, I went to the local bookstore and purchased three books on screenwriting. After reading each of them, I began to write. When I traveled I wrote. I wrote in the hotel room, and even late at night after my family went to bed. I was consumed. A few months and one hundred and twenty-five pages later, the script was complete.

We are all afforded a certain number of opportunities in life and we must act on them when they come. Are there better and more qualified writers than I? Absolutely, but I looked out and saw people who were doing it and thought to myself, "They aren't any smarter than I am." Sure, there were days when the ideas wouldn't come and I had severe writer's block. However, one day at a time, I operated from my imagination, taking one step at a time.

Every day I imagined the story I was writing and also what the completion would look like. I thought of all the opportunities that would surely come my way as a result. I imagined the doors that would open which would allow me to have greater impact on larger numbers of people worldwide. I even imagined someday walking down the Hollywood red carpet. Even if writers don't walk down the red carpet, it sure felt exciting. Using my imagination in this way enabled me to take an almost overwhelming task at times and find joy in it.

I made the decision that I would no longer talk

about my idea. I was going to put my action where my mouth was. I was going to be a doer and not a talker. I had gone from being interested in the idea to being committed to it. Does this take courage? Yes. Will there be some who will doubt you? Yes. Are you going to get resistance from people in your life? Yes. Will there be times when you feel you don't have what it takes? Yes. Remember, courage is not the absence of fear, it is the ability to feel the fear and *do it anyway*.

A young man was playing the piano late one night in a club when a patron who had been drinking came up to him and asked him to sing. The man was a regular in the club and spent a lot of money there. He told the pianist that he didn't come to the club to hear someone only playing the piano—he wanted to hear singing. The pianist looked up at him and said he was not a singer, and that he only played the piano. Consequently, the man became upset and walked over to the bartender expressing his desire to hear singing. He told the bartender that if he didn't start hearing some singing, he and his friends would leave. Immediately, the bartender walked over to this young man playing the piano and told him that if he didn't start singing, he would be fired and forced to go out and find a new job somewhere else. Although he didn't see himself as a singer, he sang anyway. And no one ever sang the song "Sweet Lorraine" like Nat King Cole.

That night was not only an eye-opener for Nat, it was a breakthrough. It had awakened the greatness he possessed within. After patrons made continual requests to hear him sing, someone at Decca Records heard his rendition and immediately wanted to sign him to the label. The rest is history.

There will be times when the ability to take action will require you to face your fears and inadequacies. At times there will be a voice inside that will try to convince you your dream is *not* possible. But like Nat King Cole, sometimes it isn't until you take action that you realize the ability, talent, and greatness you possess within.

When I was sixteen, I can remember watching motivational speakers, and wondering if I would ever have enough to say to fill an hour. Then came the time when I wondered if I would ever know enough to speak for four hours. Once I mastered four hours I wondered if I would ever have enough knowledge and experience to present a two-day seminar. I learned that once I acted on these goals, I grew; with each action, more opportunities were made available to me. I realized that I didn't have to be great to start, but in order to be great I would have to start. By doing what is wrong we often learn what is right. I had to stop expecting to be perfect and instead decide to start taking action.

The truth is that you can have all the belief, skill,

and desire in the world, but if you don't take action, nothing happens. If you are in sales and you believe in your product and yourself, yet you don't take action, it is unlikely you will sell anything. If you are unhappy with your finances, relationship, or job, but do nothing about it, then nothing will change. Jim Rohn once said, "Affirmation without discipline is the beginning of delusion." Unfortunately, many people fool themselves into believing that their ship will come in without taking any significant action. They forget that a plane is full throttle as it takes off and begins climbing the blue sky, and the pilot doesn't back off the throttle until the optimum momentum and altitude is reached.

One way to increase your ability to act is to stand up to the inner voice that causes you to live less than your true potential. If you decide that something is important to you, turn off that inner critic. I don't know if you have ever been chased by a dog before or not, but it's not exactly a pleasant experience. I can remember jogging on a few occasions when mean-looking dogs ran up attempting to chase me and even bite my leg. Since then, I have learned to stop right where I am, turn around, stare directly into the dog's eyes, walk right toward it, and in a stern and unwavering voice tell it, "Get out of here!" Nine times out of ten, dogs will immediately turn around and run off. This is how you must be with your fears and your critics. Face them with confidence. Does this take courage? Yes! Will the thought pass through your mind, "What if it doesn't work?" Yes! Again, this is all a part of the process.

When taking action on your dreams, you have to momentarily disassociate from all that could go wrong and all the reasons why something won't work. You must change your focus from what could potentially go wrong to what could be gained by taking action. In that fleeting moment of suspending fear, you must take action.

On the first success tape I ever listen to by Jim Rohn, he taught, "Always act when the emotion is high." Take action when the inspiration is present and strong. Don't allow the emotion to leave without first taking some sort of action. Great ideas and opportunities are slippery. Take advantage of these opportunities when they arise. They come at odd times and few in number. By taking action when the inspiration is strong, you begin to create momentum. Whether large or small, each action you take will give you continued motivation and a massive desire to keep going.

Sometimes you will be required to take action without clearly seeing the end result. Often the path is not clearly laid out in front of you. You cannot expect to know everything before you take action. You cannot expect to have the perfect strategy planned out before you decide to act. Action requires faith. Now, don't get me wrong. Strategy is important, but if you spend all your time strategizing and never take action, you'll remain where you are. There are times when even an effective strategy can't be formed without first taking some sort of action—even if it is a few little steps.

It can also be beneficial to break big goals down into smaller ones. If the action you are about to take creates overwhelming fear, then scale down the amount of risk and gradually increase it. In *Success through a Positive Mental Attitude*, W. Clement Stone states,

> Roger Bannister reasoned that a man ran a single quarter-mile faster than he ran the four quarters of a full mile. So he trained himself to think of the four quarters in the mile separately. In his training he would dash a quarter mile, then jog a lap around the track to rest. Then he would dash another quarter mile. Each time he aimed to run the quarter in 58 seconds or less. Fifty-eight times four equals 232 seconds, or three minutes and 52 seconds. He ran to the point of collapse. Then he would rest . . . When he finally ran his great race, it was in 3 minutes, 59. 6 seconds!

Finally, someone had broken the four-minute-mile time barrier.

Doing a little at a time is an excellent strategy that can help your confidence grow. If you want to learn how to high jump, you wouldn't start out at six feet. Maybe start out at three feet and work your way up. In mathematics you don't start out multiplying 3,494 x 26,589. You start out with 2 + 2.

Although you take action, your goals will not always unfold as you planned. When you don't get the outcome that you anticipated, make sure you are using the most effective strategy. You may possess commitment, belief, or any other principle in the book, but if you're utilizing a weak strategy, I've got news for you—success is unlikely to happen. If you want to go south and your path is taking you west, it is improbable that you will get where you want to go.

In developing or changing your strategy, be sure to take into account your timing and circumstance. The same strategy won't always work in a different set of circumstances. You must be willing to change your approach when you discover you are not producing the desired outcome. Don't be so locked onto one approach that you become inflexible. If you know that the action you are taking is not giving you the results you want, then change your strategy or approach.

I like what George Bernard Shaw said: "People are always blaming their circumstances for what they are. The people who get on in this world are the people who get up and look for the circumstances they want, and if they can't find them, make them."

Don't be fooled into believing that dreaming and

hoping are enough to get you what you want. You must be willing to put yourself on the line—to defy the odds. Once a person puts himself on the line, he realizes he is much more capable than he previously thought. Once you know what you want, commit yourself to taking action. Action leads to further motivation and desire. This momentum leads to more action. Once you have this momentum, the process of achieving your goals becomes unbelievably exciting.

Today I make the commitment to take action on these goals: ________________________________

____

____.

CHAPTER 9

Maintaining a Winning Perspective

Law #8

IN THE REAL WORLD, MOMENTS OF devastation are likely to come your way. Discouragement may creep up at the slightest miscarriage of your deeds. There isn't one person on this planet who doesn't experience misfortune—we all do. It's part of the process. Consequently, setbacks drive some people to fight harder. For others, it provides a reason to quit. The difference is all in your perspective.

Although we are unable to control every situation in our lives, we *can* control how we respond to them and what meaning we assign to an outcome. Learning to master the art of interpretation and controlling your perceptions is a precious skill regardless of how difficult situations may be.

A number of years ago I met with a well-known author and speaker who has influenced millions of people. Battling with a rare form of cancer, he was given only eighteen months to live. My idea was to capture his insight, wisdom, humor, outlook on life, and especially his battle with cancer. I asked if I could interview him and record it. I suggested that once it was produced and sold in stores I would pay him a royalty on the project. He agreed and asked that I meet back at his office in one week. Over the next week I began intently preparing my dialog, and the questions I would ask. All week I memorized and imagined how the interview would successfully unfold.

The day we agreed upon had arrived and after setting up the recording equipment, we began our interview. It went very well and was even a little emotional as he shared glimpses of his personal battle with the horrible disease. He sincerely opened up to me and shared with me many of his deep and personal feelings, of which, I was humbled. Then about an hour into the interview, I looked down and noticed I hadn't pushed the record button. I was shocked and even devastated. Immediately, I felt the blood in my body rush to my face. Although, I was embarrassed, I maintained my composure. Finally, our interview ended and I told him I would get back with him in a few weeks. I was too embarrassed to tell him what had just happened.

Walking away from that experience I had a choice as to how I could communicate this experience to myself. I could have either said, "I'm a failure," "I can't do anything right," or I could simply interpret the situation as a learning experience—one I would never make again. I chose the latter interpretation. Not long after that experience I told him what had happened, and he too had a choice as to how he would respond to it. Fortunately he also chose to see it as a learning experience—I was off the hook.

As I travel the country and share this story, it inevitably causes audiences to gasp in disbelief. Many have even approached me after hearing me share the experience and suggested that possibly it worked out just as it should have. They insist that the experience was meant for this person and myself alone. This too is a wonderful perspective.

In his book *Psycho-Cybernetics*, Maxwell Maltz says it is vital to separate who you are from your performance. Here is why this is extremely important: as someone once stated, "If you are what you do, when you don't, you aren't." In other words, if your internal communications, performance, and self-worth are all based on your performance alone, what happens when you do not perform well? Good and bad, your self-esteem and self-worth may resemble a roller coaster going up and down, rather then a constant and determined line.

Too many people allow their performance to dictate the way they feel about themselves. This is not always healthy. For example, if I give one speech out of a dozen that turns out unfavorably, that doesn't mean that I am a poor speaker. For whatever reason, it simply means that I didn't do well during that particular speech. The same is true if you set out after a goal only to find rejection and defeat. It doesn't necessarily mean that people reject you personally. If you begin taking action on a goal and fall on your face in the process, that doesn't mean that your goal isn't possible. The truth is, most goals are not accomplished overnight. In fact, the average business or idea fails a dozen times before ever finding success.

If you don't have patience with your child today, it doesn't mean that you are a bad parent. It simply means that on this day, in this situation, you aren't at your best. If you make a mistake, that doesn't mean that you personally are a mistake. If you failed at something, it doesn't mean you are a failure. Often people allow a mistake or failure in one area to bleed into other areas of their lives. They take a small event and blow it out of all reasonable proportions. Others take setbacks personal. In some cases they pity themselves or become the victim of their misfortune. Neither is healthy!

Achievers realize that there is no such thing as

failure, because they seek to grow from each setback. Although not always a comfortable experience, achievers choose to see adversities as assets rather than liabilities. Many of the great achievers have often said they were thankful for their setbacks because those experiences were viewed as a source of strength that helped prepare them for opportunities that would come next.

It is important to look for the blessings in disguise. W. Clement Stone said, "Every adversity has the seed of an equivalent or greater benefit." In these moments, you must say this to yourself and believe that something good will come of this. Then ask yourself, what is good about this problem? How can this problem benefit me? When you ask these questions, your brain will eventually find the answers. No matter how bleak, there is always a blessing in disguise. If you have been laid-off from your job, you can decide to perceive it as though there is a better opportunity elsewhere. Maybe the universe was simply helping you make a decision that you knew you needed to make but kept putting it off. This job change is now providing you an opportunity to grow. If someone in a relationship left you, possibly it is time to move on and find someone who will treat you better, someone that is right for you. Think about it, have you ever been faced with something terrible that actually turn out to be a blessing? I sure you have. It all has to do with how you look at it. Even anxiety can be good if it leads you to do something productive. Dyslexia can even be good if you can find a productive use for it. An apparent weakness can actually be a strength if you make it so. Whatever you look for you will find.

There is a story told of a young man who grew up in a poor village. When he was old enough he left the village in search of riches. The villagers were happy for him and patiently anticipated his return, because they put all their hopes for the future in him. Some years later he returned to the village. The villagers were excited to see what fortunes he had brought back. When they gathered around, he reached into his pocket and pulled out three little seeds. They scoffed and ridiculed him, complaining that his time away had been a waste. The people of the village were let down. All of the hopes and dreams they had placed in this young boy had quickly vanished. After enduring a barrage of scoffing and ridicule, the young man turned and walked to a nearby field and planted the seeds in the ground. The three seeds were cocoa seeds and as the legend goes, the main crop today in Ghana are cocoa plants because of this one young man. This man didn't see his three little seeds as failure; he saw them as the answer.

Life can be full of problems or it can be full of wonderful blessings. It is all a matter of how you look at it. Some people find difficulty in every opportunity and others find opportunity in every difficulty. Where do you lean? Even in the worst of circumstances, history shows this power in action. In his classic book *Man's Search for Meaning*, Viktor Frankl points out that many of those who survived the Nazi concentration camps said that they "benefited from the captivity, seeing it as a growth experience," although it was a horrendous time. Many came out of that experience having discovered God, themselves, and the realization that they could handle much more than they had previously thought. On the other hand, there were also those that saw their captivity differently and found ways to end their lives prematurely. The difference between the two was primarily the way they communicated internally about the experience—in other words, perspective. Whatever you focus on and the meaning you give it, will determine your experience. It's up to you.

In 1973, W. Mitchell was driving his motorbike when he was distracted and took his eyes off the road for a second too long. When he finally looked forward, he realized he was about to collide with a semi that had come to a stop in front of him. In that split second he made the decision to lay down the bike. After sliding more than one hundred feet and breaking many bones in his body, the gasoline cap popped off and spread fuel all over the ground. The motorbike caught fire, burning 65 percent of his body with third-degree burns. You would think this would be enough to experience in one lifetime, but after leaving the hospital six months later, he and three of his friends took off in an airplane. Once they reached ninety feet in the air, the plane lost power and dropped like a rock. There were four people on the plane that day and three walked away unscarred. The fourth person, W. Mitchell, was unable to move his body. His lower back was crushed, and he was paralyzed from the waist down. Unlike most people, he didn't give up or lose his zest for life. Instead he said, "Before, there were ten thousand things I could do. Now there are nine thousand. I can either dwell on the one thousand I've lost, or focus on the nine thousand things left." After these experiences, he has gone on to be a mayor, congressional nominee, gubernatorial candidate, and million dollar businessman. Today he is also a motivational speaker. This greatness lies within each of us.

Often, it is through pain that we grow the most. There are libraries full of books about men and women who have turned tragedy into triumph. Many achievers started off with very little and managed to find enormous success. Similarly, there are many who were given every opportunity, all the love and encouragement, and still they turned out broke and depressed. It is never the events or circumstances themselves that determine whether you are successful or defeated. More importantly, it is how you perceive and respond to your challenges that makes the difference.

Mastering the habit of interpreting each setback as an opportunity or blessing in disguise will give you the energy to push forward when the future looks dim. Just like no problem is permanent, each setback is not an attack on you personally. I remember there were times when in the face of setbacks all I could do was think to myself, "Well, at least one day this will make a good story." There are times when we must simply trust that the circumstances are for our good.

Remember to capitalize on small wins. Realize that you cannot run faster than you are able. But as long as you are making progress, sooner or later you will find the success you are looking for.

"Success," said IBM founder T.J. Watson, "is on the far side of failure." Even the discovery of "Post-It Notes" were born as the result of a failure. In the 1970s, chemist Spencer Silver was working for the 3M company to improve the acrylic adhesives used on their tapes. As a result of an accident, he created an adhesive that wasn't very sticky, yet wouldn't dry either. This failure gave birth to a new idea that is now used in homes and offices around the world.

It is all in how you look at it. When things don't turn out as you would like them to—as occurs from time to time—choose to see the momentary setback as an opportunity to change and grow. One of the greatest coaches of all time, John Wooden once said, "Things turn out best for those that make the best of the way things turn out."

The power of maintaining a winning perspective will give you the energy and drive to press forward despite momentary setbacks.

Today I make the choice to re-interpret and perceive my current circumstances or this specific past event in a more beneficial way: ______________________________

____

____.

CHAPTER 10

Creating Your Own Success Team

Law #9

DALE CARNEGIE USED TO TEACH THAT there is no such thing as a self-made man. In the real world, no success is achieved by a single person. No one stands alone. In the end, none of us makes it to the top by ourselves.

For this reason, achievers understand the importance of creating a home-court advantage. In order to get what you want, it will be necessary to surround yourself with people who can help you get it. You must associate with people who compensate for your weaknesses. Partner with those who are smarter than you. Create associations and friendships that you can draw upon for ideas, energy, perspective, motivation, and accountability.

Whether you study great teachers, co-workers, parents, leaders, athletes, and so on, you will find that they all had the benefit of either being mentored or influenced by other people.

Albert Einstein said, "Many times a day I realize how much my own outer and inner life is built upon the labors of my fellow men, both living and dead, and how earnestly I must exert myself in order to give in return as much as I have received."

Earlier I said that the same level of thinking that has brought you this far in your life is not enough to take you where you want to go. Making an effort to wisely and consciously choose your associations and the influences you surround yourself with can and *will* have a dramatic impact on your thinking, your beliefs, your habits, and your achievements.

Napoleon Hill spoke of the "Master Mind" principle, which he defined as "the coordination of knowledge and effort, in a spirit of harmony, between two or more people, for the attainment of a definite purpose." In his book *Think and Grow Rich,* Mr. Hill tells of Henry Ford, who became one of the wealthiest men in America in a rather short period of time.

Mr. Ford's most rapid strides became noticeable from

the time he became a personal friend of Thomas A. Edison. . . Go a step further and consider the fact that Mr. Ford's most outstanding achievements began from the time that he formed the acquaintances of Harvey Firestone, John Burroughs, and Luther Burbank . . . Through his association with Edison, Burbank, Burroughs, and Firestone, Mr. Ford added to his own brainpower the sum and substance of the intelligence, experience, knowledge, and spiritual forces of these four men.

In *The Success Principles*, Jack Canfield co-author of the *Chicken Soup for the Soul* series told of how his partnership with Mark Victor Hansen began. While having breakfast one morning Mark asked Jack, "What are you up to? What are you excited about?"

Jack proceeded to tell him about the *Chicken Soup* idea. Immediately, Mark said, "I want to be your partner on this book. I want to help you write it."

Jack replied, "Mark, the book is already half written. Why would I let you be my partner at this stage of the project?"

"Well," he replied, "a lot of stories you tell, you learned from me. I have a lot more you haven't heard. I know I can get great stories from lots of other motivational speakers, and I can help you market the book to people and places you've probably never even thought of."

As they continued to talk, Jack realized that Mark

would be a great asset to the project. So they struck a deal. After selling almost 100 million *Chicken Soup* books worldwide, Jack went on to say that as a result of that one conversation, it has been worth tens of millions in book royalties and licensing income to Mark and himself. The same can happen for you. The same can happen for you. Unforeseen power and opportunities will arise when you spend the majority of time with the right people.

Our environment and those with whom we associate will have a profound impact on who we become and how much we achieve. The natural world also demonstrates this effect. For example, look at the ways in which certain species of fish grow according to their environment. Put them in a small aquarium and they remain small even into adulthood. Release them into a larger body of water and they grow to their full intended size. Human achievement appears to function the same way.

Attitudes, demeanor, and energy are contagious. Like a sickness, if you want the flu, hang around people that have the flu. You've heard the phrase "Lie down with dogs and you come up with fleas." If you are not the kind of person who steals, hang around people who steal and watch what happens. As a result of your surrounding influences, you may just give in, and sooner or later you may be stealing too. People eventually wear down. Slowly, your beliefs may change, and you begin believing that it is okay to steal.

You may be the fastest runner in the world, but if you are running in quicksand, you'll be hindered and never set the record you are capable of achieving. Likewise, if you spend time with the wrong people, their influence could prevent you from maximizing your potential.

In general there are two types of people and the dominant attitudes they possess: those who are positive and those who are negative. To get the most out of yourself, it is vital that you spend your time with positive people.

Positive people are those who take charge of problems rather than complain about them. They don't criticize. They have the tendency to look for the good in people and their situation. They are solution-oriented. They make an effort to minimize problems rather than enlarge them. They keep their eye on the big picture, making the best out of each situation and even asking for learning opportunities. They seek to squeeze lemonade from the lemons of life!

Good things seem to happen to positive people. They seldom get depressed and rarely cause others to become discouraged or depressed. When you share your goals with them, they are naturally supportive. They are happy, which makes them pleasant to be around. They smile and cause others to do the same. If you were to name the five people you admired most, I'm quite certain they would represent one or more of these characteristics.

I suspect you have also been around people who were just the opposite; people who are negative, cynical, or even destructive. These people have been identified as "toxic" people. They lack faith and they criticize. They are the people who drain and drag you down. It is their mission to tell you how and why things can't be done. The more you strive to succeed the more they strive to prevent success from happening. It may not always be noticeable. They may be subtle, sitting back and even snickering. The moment you make a mistake, they are quick to point it out.

Although you are responsible for your own emotions, these people can cause you to feel stressed, insecure, and even sick inside. If you spend much time with them, they can impact your blood pressure and your health. When hard times come, they blame others rather than take responsibility. They complain when things don't go their way, quickly determining that their failures are someone else's fault. All of this leads them to the dangerous spiral of the victim mentality.

If you find yourself associating with negative people, my advice is to turn, run, and never look back. Charles "Tremendous" Jones had a phrase that he often shared: "You will be the same person in five years that you are today except for the people you meet and the books you read." If you find yourself surrounded by people who are destructive, let them go. It is not worth the price.

Lee Iacocca understood this and applied it when he took the helm as CEO of the Chrysler Corporation and saved the company from bankruptcy. In his biography he stated that in his first thirty-six months at Chrysler, he replaced thirty-five out of thirty-six senior vice presidents. He went on to say that this made all the difference. This may sound harsh, but it's true. If you have people who are standing in your way, get them out of your sphere of influence.

Granted, I know you are probably thinking that you can't, because it's your spouse, co-worker, or good friend who is negative. If this is the case then you have three options to consider. The first is to be a leader and inspire them through your example. Dr. Phil says, "We teach people how to treat us by our own actions and behaviors." The second is to spend as little time as possible with this person. Third, keep your goals and dreams quietly hidden from them. W. Clement Stone said, "Confide in no one but those that have genuine sympathy with your cause and an understanding of your possibilities. Otherwise, keep your plans to yourself and let your actions speak." If there is a family dinner or a social function that you would like to attend, then attend, but don't include them in your goals and dreams. You don't need their approval anyway!

I am not suggesting that you align yourself only with people who like you and believe in you. Yes, having these people in your life is important, but there is something more. It is important to associate with those who add to your reservoir; people who cause you to stretch to be better. If you want to become a great tennis player, you wouldn't play with someone who has less skill than you or even equal skill if you plan on becoming great.

Get around people who challenge and support you. J. Willard Marriott, founder of Marriott Hotels had a statement that he lived by: "Good timber does not grow with ease. The stronger the wind the stronger the trees." The great quarterback Steve Young once spoke on the concept of influence and his association with Joe Montana. He said that even though he was offered contracts to play on other teams as the starting quarterback, he rejected them because of the value he gained by playing under the great Joe Montana. He said that if he were going to be the best, he had to associate with the best.

At an early age Steven Spielberg spent his days at Universal Studios watching directors and film crews. He followed them around asking questions, desiring to learn all that he possibly could—which eventually led the directors to ask for his input. He also studied the work of Martin Scorsese and Francis Ford Coppola. Eventually he found kinship with George Lucas, who said, "We were always willing to help each other make the best movie." Steven Spielberg spent the majority of his time with those who could not only help him grow, but also provide a different perspective, knowledge, experience, and intelligence.

Align yourself with those who are qualified. If you want to be a millionaire, it wouldn't be wise to take advice from someone who doesn't have a dollar in his bank account. Get around other millionaires. If you want to own your own business, associate with people who are successful at running their own businesses.

Surround yourself with people who have vast experience in your area of interest. In the beginning you may not know anyone who can provide this level of mentoring, or you may not yet have become the type of person who will attract such a mentor. Thus, your mentors and influences will be the books you read, the audio programs you listen to, and the seminars you attend. In fact, did you know that the average person commutes 30 minutes each way, both to and from work? What is even more surprising fact is that the total time commuting in one year is 1,250 hours. This is enough time to give yourself a college education. In a few short years, it is enough time to become an expert at virtually any area of expertise you choose.

These resources make wonderful mentors, providing you with great ideas, motivation, confidence, knowledge, and greater belief in yourself and your possibilities. Anthony

Robbins said, "No matter how grim your world is, if you can read about the accomplishments of others, you can create the beliefs that will allow you to succeed."

Geese are excellent examples of creating a success team. Have you ever noticed that geese fly in a V formation? Have you ever wondered why that is and what benefit it provides? Some time ago I came across research which concluded that as each goose flaps its wings it creates an "uplift" for the birds that follow. This strategy allows each bird to save 50 percent of its energy by reducing the drag. As a result geese can fly 71 percent farther as a group in this formation than one can fly alone. The same is true of people. If you want to see your future- look at the people with whom you spend most of your time. The people you consistently associate with will have a dramatic impact on where you end up in life.

When people can't see possibility for themselves, they most likely can't see it for you either. Thus, limit your contact and associations with those who stand in the way of achieving all that you can. On the other hand, some people see far more possibility and potential in you than you do. These are the type of people you want to be associated with.

Make the commitment today that you will develop yourself in such a way that you will begin to attract people into your life who will greatly contribute to the achievement of your goals.

Below is a list of those individuals I desire to associate with. The team I want to create that will contribute to the achievement of my most important goals includes: ______

____

____

____.

CHAPTER 11

The Power of Focus

Law #10

ONE MAJOR REASON PEOPLE NEVER GET what they want is because they lose focus on what is most important. Og Mandino said, "Too many of us never realize our greatness because we get sidetracked by secondary activity." We decide to go after a goal, and before you know it we start "majoring in minor things." We start dabbling a little over here and a little over there, and wind up never getting closer to achieving our goals. You've probably heard it said, "A man with one watch always knows what time it is. A man with two watches is never quite sure."

Achievers make a conscious effort to stay focused on those things that can really make a difference in their goals and lives. This can be difficult at times. We live in a world that is consistently vying for our energy and attention. From the moment we get up, advertising bombards us through the television, the Internet, E-mails, and even the telephone.

We are motivated by the desire to experience pleasure and avoid pain. Because we all want to be happy, we sometimes spread ourselves thin by engaging in these pleasurable, yet unproductive activities. If we are not careful, we may unknowingly trade in what we want for the moment, for what we want long-term. Be wise when spending time and energy in relationships, sports, hobbies, work and other activities or commitments. They may stand in the way of getting what you really want.

Achievers know that if they are going to accomplish anything of value they will need to concentrate all their energies. Concentration and focus provide an enormous power. Sunlight, when focused through a magnifying glass, will set a leaf on fire. Although the same sun may have been shining down on the leaf all day, the effect was not as powerful until the sunlight was focused and concentrated. The same is true with your goals. When all of your resources are focused on a single purpose, only then do you have the combining power to get what you want.

Les Brown tells of a baseball team that was at the bottom of the league. That year a new coach was hired. The first thing the coach did was ask the pitcher, "What is your best throw?" The pitcher said, "I've got a good fastball, curveball, and knuckleball." The coach responded, "No, what is your best throw?" The pitcher replied he had a great fastball. The coach immediately told him, "That's all I want you to work on this whole season—your fastball." Les points out that this team went from the bottom of the league to the World Series.

Concentration and focus means that you walk a straight line until the goal is accomplished. Charles Dickens said, "I could have never done it without . . . the determination to concentrate myself on one subject at a time."

Trying to be a jack of all trades often leads to being a master of none. Wearing too many hats, if not properly managed, can eventually become a definite obstacle keeping you from achieving your goals. A world champion tennis player doesn't get to that level by playing miniature golf. Likewise, a world-class stockbroker doesn't get to the highest level of his profession by spending time socializing around the office water cooler.

In the beginning, there might be a time and a place to take on many roles. When I first started my business,

I was manager, graphic designer, salesman, recording engineer, and presenter—which included traveling. There is a time and place for everything. However, there came a time when the demands of all these roles took their toll and prevented the business from growing at my desired rate. Realizing this, I began delegating anything that was not necessary for me to do myself.

In 1895, after studying the distribution of wealth in Italy, Vilfredo Pareto, an Italian economist, concluded that eighty percent of Italy's wealth was controlled by twenty percent of the people, and that twenty percent of the wealth was controlled by the other eighty percent. In the 1920s and 1930s Dr. Joseph M. Juran studied and coined the concept as the 80/20 rule or the Pareto Principle.

Twenty percent of any group produces eighty percent of the overall results. This is true of you as well; twenty percent of all you do will usually have a greater impact than the other eighty percent combined. Be sure that your thoughts and actions are focused on the top twenty percent of all your activities. If you have ten activities in front of you that need your attention, concentrate on the top two that will provide the greatest payoff. This will account for eighty percent of your overall results.

After interviewing two million achievers over the last fifty years, Marcus Buckingham wrote in his popular book *Now, Discover Your Strengths,* "People who were truly successful in their chosen profession, from teaching to telemarketing, acting to accounting—discovered that the secret to their success was in their ability to discover their strengths, and to organize their life so that those strengths could be applied."

When pursuing your goals, spend most of your time engaging in your areas of strength. Jack Canfield teaches, "Identify your core genius, then delegate completely to free up more time to focus on what you love to do." If bookkeeping is not your strength, hire or team up with someone else who can do it. If you are great at starting projects but weak at completing them, align yourself with people that are strong on finishing tasks. Determining your priorities and then drawing upon your strengths will be a major step toward success.

As I work with supervisors in organizations, it often becomes apparent that some leaders find it difficult to "let go" and delegate. It doesn't allow the organization to grow and mature. Many leaders possess the belief that "I can get the job done right and do it faster if I handle it myself. Also, I won't need to spend the time training someone else how to do it." The problem with this belief and style of leadership is that it often leads the manager's employees to feel that they or their abilities are not trusted. More importantly, it doesn't allow for the leader's greatest strengths to be applied at their optimum level.

Great leaders prefer investing a good amount of their time in the beginning to train a subordinate how to do a particular task. As a result, once the individual is properly trained, the leaders' time is relied less upon. This in turn, frees up the leader to put his time in more effective areas.

At times, keeping your eye completely focused will require you to say "no" or "let go" of roles that may be standing in the way. Stephen Covey reported that the late J. C. Penney believed the "wisest decision he ever made was to 'let go' after realizing he couldn't do it by himself any longer." Ask yourself if what you are doing right now is directly helping you achieve your goals. If you realize your strategy or actions are taking you in the wrong direction, change them.

There may come a time when you will need to make sacrifices. If being a member of a board is standing in your way, resign. If game night is taking too much time away from more important things, dismiss yourself. Taking on too many activities and roles can steal the necessary time and energy needed to master your craft.

It is important that you avoid anything that stands in your way or dilutes your energies. I remind you that this book is designed for people who want to achieve. One definite rule of achievement is, once you know what you want, get single-minded and stay single minded until you have achieved your goals.

Today I will eliminate or reduce these activities from my life: ______________________________________

____

____

Today I will put the majority of my focus in this area:

____

____

______________________________________.

CHAPTER 12

Creating a Sense of Urgency

Law #11

THE TRUTH IS THAT YOU DON'T HAVE A thousand years to live. In life, you are not afforded the luxury of unlimited time or a watch that lets you know how many days, months, or years you have left. For this reason, begin living with a sense of urgency—a sense that now is the time to start living your dreams.

Many, if not most people, are living their lives by the credo "I'll do it tomorrow, next month, or next year." "One of these days I'll do it." They imagine it will be easier to take action in the future than it will be to take action today. Once that day arrives, they are still standing at first base. How many people do you know that have great ideas and abilities but continue to put off taking action? What about you? What ideas or goals do you have, that you continue putting off?

Life truly is just a flicker. You are here one day and gone the next. There are no guarantees that tomorrow will arrive, and yet the average person watches 6.5 hours of television per day.

Some people wait around hoping that their knight in shining armor will arrive. If you are waiting for someone to hand you your dreams, I've got news for you, it's not going to happen! Life is not that easy. And it is this attitude that causes so many to "go to their graves with their music still in them," as Oliver Wendell Holmes put it. Many people have great intentions and ideas, but those alone won't take you very far. You actually have to do something and, more importantly, you have to do it *now*.

Stop waiting for your circumstances to improve before you act. When opportunities reveal themselves—as they will from time to time—you mustn't let them pass without acting. The world is constantly changing and evolving. The pace of life is so much faster than ever before. It used to be that you had years before your business competition caught up to you. Today, you may barely have months over your competition—if you are lucky. Stop procrastinating!

While in my early twenties, I looked for ways to increase my credibility and value before I set out to live my dream, which was to provide ideas and tools that could improve the quality of people's lives. One day some entrepreneurs asked me to help them start a business. They informed me that they had an idea that had not been put to the test in a particular region of the United States. After taking a few days to think about it and calculate the risks involved, I decided it was the time to act. Desire and opportunity had collided. I left my job working for a senator in Washington, D. C. and went to Utah. Within a year the business took off successfully.

A few years later, the same group with whom I had started the business came to me with a new idea for a second business. I accepted that opportunity and within a short period of time it became a multi million-dollar company. In each case it was important to act immediately. Had I waited, the opportunity would have passed by. This became evident when I noticed that it didn't take long before other companies started duplicating our ideas. As a result of acting when we did, however, we were able to maintain, an edge in the marketplace.

In his book *Paradigms*, Joel Barker points out that in 1968, Switzerland dominated the world in watchmaking. In fact, the Swiss held 65 percent of the market place and more than 80 percent of the profits. For over one hundred years they were known for their watchmaking excellence. Then, within a mere ten years, their market share plummeted to less than 10 percent, leading to layoffs of fifty thousand out of their sixty-five thousand employees within three years.

Today America and Japan dominate the world of watchmaking. Joel asks the question, "How did the switch happen? Why did the Swiss, who dominated so massively, lose it almost overnight?" Because their beliefs prevented them from acting urgently on their new discovery. They were so confident in their mechanical watches that when the quartz watch, which was totally electronic and one thousand times more accurate was presented, they didn't act on it.

The Swiss thought no one would want a watch without gears, bearings, or a main spring. They were so confident, they didn't even protect the idea. The Swiss openly displayed the idea to the world at the Annual Watch Conference and both Texas Instruments and Seiko took one look at it, and the rest is history.

The same thing happened when Howard Schultz came up with his idea for the espresso bar café. He had recently returned from a business trip in Italy and was impressed with their rich flavored espressos and the way they were served. He was also impressed by the intimate relationship between café employees and their customers.

When he returned to the U. S., he brought this idea back with him, but the owners of the organization he was working for at the time, a wholesale coffee company, didn't see the merit in his discovery. Consequently, he left the organization and started his own business. Today, Starbucks Coffee is one of the most successful companies in the U. S., with over seven thousand stores and new ones opening every day. What is even more amazing to think of are the thousands of people who had also visited Italy and had been equally impressed, but didn't have the vision and sense of urgency to act on it.

Howard Schultz said,

> I realized what I had to do. This is my moment, I thought. If I don't seize the opportunity, if I don't step out of my comfort zone and risk it all, if I let too much time tick on, my moment will pass. I knew that if I didn't take advantage of this opportunity, I would replay it in my mind for my whole life, wondering: What if? Why didn't I? This was my shot. Even if it didn't work out, I still had to try it . . . It's one thing to dream, but when the moment is right, you've got to be willing to leave what's familiar and go out to find your own sound. That's what I did in 1985. If I hadn't, Starbucks wouldn't be what it is today.

Urgency is often confused with what is really important. What most people feel urgent about is often not important at all. If you acted urgently on every whim or desire, you would spread yourself too thin. When I speak of living with a sense of urgency, I am speaking of acting urgently once you know what you want, after having developed an effective plan, and knowing your priorities. I am not suggesting that you—fire—ready—aim. Although there may be times when it is important to do so.

For example, when it comes to deciding that you have greatness within, you should act urgently. Not much planning is necessary for that one. Deciding that you are going to live with purpose would be another decision that you could act on urgently. Once you are clear about what you want and have determined your highest priorities in relationship to your goal, take action NOW! Don't put it off another day.

When it comes to time, high achievers don't complain about the long hours; they complain that the hours aren't long enough. They are striving to fill their time completely and effectively. In a *Fortune* magazine article, several of the most successful and highly paid executives in America were interviewed about their beliefs in relationship to time. The average yearly income among those interviewed was $1,380,000, and each had worked his way up from entry-level positions. When asked about time, they all saw time as a scarce resource and thus used their time very carefully. Benjamin Franklin said, "Do you love life? Then do not squander time, for that's the stuff life is made of."

This doesn't mean you have to become a workaholic. Achievers realize that there are other important things in life, and they give attention to them. However, when it comes to achieving their goals, they recognize they don't have an unlimited supply of time. They simply choose not to waste time on meaningless activities.

After his embezzling conviction, William Sydney Porter didn't just sit in his prison cell twiddling his thumbs. He decided to write short stories and did so under the name of O. Henry. By the time he walked out of prison, he was one of the most popular short-story writers in the country.

If you have ideas, goals, and dreams within you waiting to be unleashed, start living with a sense of urgency. The inventions we know Thomas Edison by today were created after his sixtieth birthday. Norman MaClean and Grandma Moses decided to act despite their advanced age. There are examples of thousands of others, all at different stages in their lives, both young and old, who began living with urgency. This urgency not only enabled them to achieve their goals, but it also allowed them to make a contribution to their family, community, country, and even the world.

Today—this moment—is the only time you are

guaranteed. There is no guarantee tomorrow will come. There is no guarantee the same opportunities that reveal themselves today will be around tomorrow. The Pulitzer Prize–winning composer Gian Carlo Menotti said, "Hell begins on that day when God grants us a clear vision of all that we might have achieved, of all the gifts we wasted, of all that we might have done that we did not do." Stop living your life like you have a thousand years to live. Stop procrastinating, and start acting!

Today I will begin going after these three goals with a greater sense of urgency:

1. ______________________________.

2. ______________________________.

3. ______________________________.

CHAPTER 13

Never Give Up

Law #12

QUITTING IS EASY. When things get difficult, most people simply give up. They don't have the vision or discipline to keep going when the going gets tough. History books are filled with countless stories of both men and women who knew the importance of perseverance and of the warnings of those who gave up! In fact, many described their failures and defeats as necessary stepping-stones toward their success.

Did you know that Walt Disney was turned down 302 times before the banks lent him the money to build Disneyland? Walt had a vision and stayed committed to fulfilling it. He realized that although he would encounter rejection, if he didn't give up on his vision, it wouldn't give up on him. Had this not been the case, millions each year wouldn't have the good fortune of experiencing "The Happiest Place on Earth."

Before Howard Schultz founded Starbucks Coffee, he spoke to 242 investors and all but 17 turned him down. Most of the 242 prospective investors told Howard that it was a crazy idea. But that didn't stop him.

Colonel Sanders was in his sixties when he decided his social security check wasn't enough to live on and went out to market his great idea. What was it? A chicken recipe that he thought everyone would want. He went from restaurant to restaurant asking if they would use his chicken recipe, and they thought he, too, was crazy. The owners of the restaurants told him time and time again that they already had a chicken recipe, and they didn't need his. Finally, after hundreds of rejections somebody said Yes, and Kentucky Fried Chicken was born.

When we think of Thomas Edison, did you know that in the process of inventing the light bulb he encountered over 9,999 failures? He said, "Genius is one percent inspiration and ninety-nine percent perspiration!"

In the beginning, Dr. Seuss was rejected by twenty-eight publishers. The publishers considered the books "too outlandish to appeal to children." Abraham Lincoln spent most of his life failing before he became president of the United States. In its first 28 attempts to send a rocket into space, NASA failed 20 times. Would you have kept trying after hundreds of failures? Unfortunately, most people wouldn't. Most people would have given up long before 302 – 242 – 28 or even a dozen failures. In fact, most people give up after one or two setbacks.

There is one guaranteed way you won't fulfill your dreams, and that is to simply quit on them. Unfortunately, most people do. The classic film, *Chariots of Fire,* depicts athletes competing against one another, their sacrifice and motivation. One of the athletes, Harold Abrahams, while competing for a position on the British team, lost several heats against a Scottish runner. Abrahams complained to his girlfriend, "If I can't win—I won't run!" His girlfriend responded sharply, "If you don't run you can't win."

Most people throw in the towel too soon. Had they given one more last effort and a little more time, they may have seen the harvest of their labors. We live in a culture of immediate gratification. It's a disease that causes us to think, if I can't have it now, it either isn't worth it or it must not be possible.

It's wonderful to expect to be a winner; in fact, it is necessary—but don't expect to start out being one. Before you can become great at anything, it is likely that you will first be awful. Developing a skill or achieving a goal will be difficult at first. Furthermore, your goals don't always unfold exactly how you imagine they would. Consequently, people get discouraged when the results don't match their internal picture and expectations.

Although many of the success stories you are familiar with may seem to have been instant successes, you don't always see the years of preparation and the many setbacks that contributed to their success. No matter the goal, results are produced much like compounding interest. You won't see any significant growth day to day, but progress is being made. A. L. Williams said, "Ninety percent of businesses fail because most people get out of business before they give their efforts time to compound."

If you believe in your goals strongly enough, and if you are committed to them, they will eventually bear fruit. Anything that is given consistent attention will grow.

I've seen countless times when a salesperson finally summoned the courage to knock on a door or approach a prospect only to find rejection and immediately decide they weren't meant to be a salesperson. Yet, on a number of occasions, just as the salesperson was about to give up, I would encourage them to contact one more person or knock on a few more doors and usually they would get the sale.

The unfortunate thing about giving up is that after you give up once, it becomes easier to do it a second time.

This can lead to a third time and before you know it, you have made it a habit. Vince Lombardi, speaking in the locker room to one of his players said, "If you quit now, during these workouts, you'll quit in the middle of the season in a game. Once you learn to quit, it becomes a habit. We don't want anyone who will quit. We want 100 percent out of each individual, and if you don't want to give it, get out. Just get up and get out right now." You don't want it to be said of you that you were a quitter. You don't want to look in the mirror and think, "If I had just held on and pushed myself a little longer and a little harder I could have made it." If you are not careful, quitting can become a way of life.

Develop the habit of following through. Someone said, "Stopping at third base adds no more to the score than striking out." If you have made a habit of giving up in the past, it is not too late to change. You can start by setting small goals for yourself and following through. As each goal is reached, you become satisfied, and it will motivate you to set another goal and eventually you will begin forming the new habit of following through and persevering.

You can't get away from failure and rejection if you want to make something of yourself. This is life, and it happens to all of us from time to time. This is why learning to master your internal communication is extremely vital.

You can't always control the events that take place in your life, but you can control what you do about them. Here are a few thoughts that can help.

In my seminars I teach that failure is only the end if you let it be. Keep in mind, failure is simply life's way of telling you to change your approach—to try something new. Sometimes nature has to step in to help because we don't always know what's best for ourselves. Pay attention to the feedback you are receiving. Just as Darwin taught, "only the fittest survive." In this case, the "fittest" are those who don't quit, but change their approach according to the feedback. If you stay true to the vision, always looking for a way, a better strategy, continually in pursuit of what you want, you will eventually come though. Alexander Graham Bell said, "What this power is I cannot say. All that I know is that it exists, and it becomes available only when a man or woman is in that state of mind in which he or she knows exactly what he or she wants and is fully determined not to quit—until they find it." Failure is only the end when you decide to throw in the towel and give up. Otherwise, use failures as learning opportunities, bringing you closer to your desired outcome.

One major cause of failure is the expectation of failure. Expectations control your life, so be clear about your expectations. Muhammad Ali didn't become great because he affirmed victory by stating, "*If* I win the fight," rather, he spoke in terms of "*When* I win the fight."

It is important that you keep your eye on the big picture. Imagine having already accomplished your goal and experiencing ahead of time how that feels. Your reasons will keep you going when others are giving up. Go one more step and take action, even if it is small. Each act followed through carries with it the feedback that is necessary for further motivation.

Even while I was writing this book, there were days I felt stuck and the ideas wouldn't come. There were days when I had no motivation to write. Each time I would take a moment, sometimes listening to music to help me get into the zone, and I would imagine the benefits of having a finished book. Most days this would help. Other days I simply had to discipline myself to begin writing, and eventually the desire and ideas would come. Even on the other end of the spectrum I found that there were times when I would imagine my long-term disappointment if I didn't follow through. That also seemed to help. If done carefully and periodically this too can provide the necessary drive.

Once you have the momentum—keep it going. You don't have time to relax. Bob Moawad says, "You don't want to coast unless you intend to go downhill." For you it may mean maintaining your momentum for thirty days, six months, a year, or even ten years, depending on your goal.

Sometimes you won't be able to see what lies ahead. Sometimes you'll question yourself. Sometimes you'll look into the tunnel, and you won't be able to tell whether you see the light at the other end of the tunnel or a train coming right toward you. Sometimes you get confused and maybe a little discouraged because you can't see a solution. This is all part of the process.

No matter how difficult it may get, or how discouraging it may seem, just hang on because success is right around the corner. It is much like what Chuck Yeager experienced firsthand. He was the first person to break the sound barrier. When he was forty thousand feet in the sky and approaching the sound barrier, the rocket-powered X-1 fighter plane began to vibrate as though it was about to fall apart in midair. Although the thought passed through the minds of the controllers on the ground to abort the mission, it was simply not an option. Then, just as he and others thought the plane was about to fall apart, Yeager broke through the sound barrier and immediately thereafter, the ride became smooth. The noises and vibrations ceased. Sometimes you will think you are *breaking down* and can't handle it anymore. Maybe what is really happening is that you are about to *break through*.

If you really want something important, it will often take great persistence. Only those who persevere win the prize. If you fall down, get back up and try again. Michael Jordan once said, "I've missed more than 9,000 shots in my career. I've lost almost 300 games. On 26 occasions, I have been entrusted to take the game winning shot . . . and missed. I have failed over and over and over again in my life and that's why . . . I succeed."

Today I will reaffirm to myself that I will endure and persist until this goal is achieved: ______________________

____

____.

CHAPTER 14

Live with Purpose

Law #13

IMAGINE PEOPLE YOU KNOW WHO ARE living life without any purpose and direction. Whatever the image is, I'm sure it is not very attractive.

You see, without a purpose in life, it is easy to get side tracked. Without purpose you would wander aimlessly through life. You would give up on your goals and dreams. Without purpose and desire every principle in this book is virtually worthless. Achievers understand the importance of living with a purpose. They know why they are here and they structure their life around that purpose. It gives them strength and causes them to look forward to each new day. Achievers have a certain sense and energy about themselves. They are not merely trying to get *through* life; they are striving to get the most *from* life. They strive to become the most that they can possibly be.

Achievers have a *can-do* spirit about them. They have the habit of finding reasons why things can work rather than why they can't. George Bernard Shaw said, "You see things and ask, why? But I dream of things that never were and ask, why not?" It is a beautiful thing when the spark is ignited and a vision is born.

People who have a purpose for their lives have hope for their futures. George Burns was a great example of this. In fact, his hundredth birthday party was sold out years before he turned one hundred! When President John F. Kennedy said, "In this decade we will put men on the moon," immediately the engineers and scientists started showing up for work earlier than normal and staying later. A new purpose and vision had changed the culture of their organization.

Many people lose their passion for life. If you believe this has happened to you, there comes a time when you must question your present circumstances and decide that you deserve more. That's exactly what happened to John and Peter Kockelman, who became the "incredible bungee brothers." Bungee jumping is the sport where you jump off a bridge attached to a cord and free-fall until you are snatched from death at the last second before hitting the ground. Before the Kockelman brothers were bungee jumpers, they were average Americans. Peter, the older brother, was an engineer, and John was a computer consultant. They had always wanted to start a business together. According to *Outside Magazine*, John saw his first bungee jump on a show called *That's Incredible*. John called his brother and suggested that they jump off a 140-foot bridge at the Don Pedro reservoir near Yosemite Park. Peter agreed and afterward called it "the most intense thrill I had ever experienced in my life. I felt like a spider dropping into the Grand Canyon on a thread." One year later, the younger brother, John, quit his job and decided to start a bungee-jumping business. He called Peter and urged, "Come on . . . that is not what you are on this earth for, to sit there and be calm and sit and die slowly." Peter, the cautious one, was apprehensive but said, "The saddest thing I ever saw was the engineers who I worked with who had stayed thirty years beyond the time that they should have gone out and pursued a dream. So I decided to go for it." They chose to live their dreams and Bungee Adventures was born.

Howard Schultz, of Starbucks Coffee Company, embodied this inner need and purpose when he ventured out on his own and created one of America's most successful companies. He said, "I saw the move as consistent with my life's dream, my earliest desires to do something for myself and for my family, to achieve something unique, to be in control of my own destiny."

What is your destiny? What is your purpose? What is it that you want? What are your greatest interests? Maybe it's singing or writing a book. Maybe it's dancing, acting, or starting your own business. Perhaps you want to leave your job, return home and raise your children. What are you enthusiastic about? When asked the secret to his success, Mark Twain replied, "I was born excited." Thomas Edison said, "When a man dies, if he can pass enthusiasm along to his children, he has left them an estate of incalculable value." Emerson also observed, "Every great and commanding moment in the annals of the world is the triumph of somebody's enthusiasm."

Whatever your goal is, I challenge you to go after it with everything you have. Am I suggesting that you immediately quit your job? Not necessarily! What I am suggesting is that if you choose to stay where you are, then decide that you are going to make a difference by setting a high standard for yourself that others will follow.

I feel sorry for so many who have given up and lost their zeal for life. Apathy annoys me! I once heard a line in a movie that has always stuck with me. A boy talking to his friend in the back of the school bus said, "If you sit in the back of the bus too long, you'll think you belong there."

There are people all around us who die at thirty-five, yet are buried at seventy-five. It has been said that age has more to do with your psychology than it has to do with your chronology. Some of the oldest people I know are vibrant, healthy, and passionate. Yet, some of the youngest people I know are drained of energy—barely making it out of bed. I don't know what side of the fence you are on, but I hope you have determined that something in your life is worth going after.

I believe that living without purpose can be a major cause of unhappiness and even depression. People show up for work and occupy themselves by fixing their eyes on the clock. "One more hour until lunch, fifteen minutes until break." They do just enough to prevent themselves from being fired. Most people spend their whole lives living this way. The only thing they look forward to is their paycheck at the end of the week and the weekend that follows. I suppose you can't change everybody. Some people are content with being average. But *you* are not average. You wouldn't be reading this book if you were.

On the very real far side of living without purpose or striving to live a stress free life, is death. Research indicates that the average person who retires at age sixty-five dies within three years of retirement. Why? In addition to having no genuine sense of purpose, he is not continually growing, learning, or stretching, which I believe plays a significant role in keeping the brain alive and the body vibrant.

Acting on your purpose is the key that leads to happiness, fulfillment and satisfaction. Have you ever noticed that the word satisfaction ends with the word *a-c-t-i-o-n*? In Latin, the word *satis* means "enough." The ancient Romans knew that enough action would produce satisfaction.

Earlier I mentioned that without purpose none of the principles in this book would be applied effectively. If you don't have purpose, why would you push yourself so hard? Why would you raise your standards? Why would you expect anything more than what you've accomplished in the past? You certainly wouldn't take the time to work on yourself and master your thoughts. Without purpose, life is slow and boring. Developing a real sense of purpose for your overall life is probably the greatest investment you can make.

In order to get and keep the spark you must become like a child and dream again. Imagine all the possibilities. The size of your vision is not as important as your belief in it and your commitment to it. Nonetheless, I do believe that BIG goals and visions will impact your entire life in a profound and positive way. I like what Andrew Carnegie, the richest man in the early 1900s once said, "If you want to be happy, set a goal that commands your thoughts, liberates your energy, and inspires your hopes." In the end, your purpose and big visions will be the fuel that will enable you to endure the hard times without giving up.

Mike Vance tells a story about the day Walt Disney died. While Walt lay on the hospital bed, while outside the room were a number of reporters who were trying to get what would be Walt's last interview. Security was tight, and for obvious reasons, the reporters were not allowed in. But somehow one reporter was persistent enough and eventually got into the room. Walt gestured for him to lie down next to him on the bed. His energy was very low, and he could barely speak beyond a whisper. As the reporter lay there, Walt began pointing to the ceiling in an effort to describe in detail what Epcot and Walt Disney World would look like, an amusement park that wasn't scheduled to be built for another six years. Even on his deathbed, he focused on his purpose and was sharing his dream.

At birth we were all given special and individual gifts, talents, and capabilities. We were entrusted with these gifts and encouraged to nurture them. Stephen Covey in *The 8th Habit* wonderfully states,

> Latent and undeveloped the seeds of greatness were planted. We were given magnificent birth gifts, talents, capacities, privileges, intelligences, opportunities that

> would remain largely unopened except through our own decision and effort. Because of these gifts, the potential within an individual is tremendous, even infinite. We really have no idea what a person is capable of ... The more we use and magnify our present talents, the more talents we are given and the greater our capacity becomes.

Begin living with purpose today and applying the principles described in this book. You deserve it. No, I didn't say you are entitled to it, but you will deserve it if you pay the price. Not only will it benefit you, it benefits those around you, too. I love what Nelson Mandela said when he quoted Marianne Williamson in his inaugural speech as president of South Africa,

> We ask ourselves, who am I to be brilliant, gorgeous, talented, and fabulous? Actually, who are you not to be? You are a child of God. Your playing small doesn't serve the world. There is nothing enlightened about shrinking so that other people won't feel insecure around you. We were born to make manifest the glory of God that is within us. It's not just in some of us; it's in everyone. As we let our own light shine, we unconsciously give others permission to do the same.

This is greatness.

Living with purpose doesn't mean you have to conquer the world. Yet, it doesn't mean that you play small either. It only means you live life to the fullest, striving to be the best that you can possibly be. Novelist Robert Louis Stevenson wrote, "To be what we are, and to become what we are capable of becoming, is the only end in life."

All the inspirational books and audio tapes in the world won't do anything for you if you are not first passionate, committed, and persistent. Go forward with a purpose, and unleash your individual greatness.

Jim Rohn called it *The Challenge.* "Let others lead small lives, but not you. Let others argue over small things, but not you. Let others cry over small hurts, but not you. Let others leave their future in someone else's hands, but not you."

No, not you. You are different. You are special. You are unstoppable.

When I imagine living life with purpose, what do I see? In what way will I begin living with a greater sense of purpose? How will I be different? How will I begin contributing? What inner gift will I begin developing? ____

____

____

Conclusion

Congratulations! You have finished reading *If You Think You Can!* It contains thirteen of the most important laws of not only achievement, but also life. Hopefully, you have either discovered for the first time, or been reminded of, the tools that will help you to tap the greatness you possess within. No matter how bleak or dim your circumstances or past may look, achievement is still possible for you.

Here is one last suggestion: READ IT AGAIN. Yes! Read the entire book or at the very least, review your notes and markings. Become familiar with each principle until they are all seared into your mind, both your conscious and unconscious minds. Read it once a month over the next year and I promise you, that what you have achieved today will be insignificant compared to what you'll have achieved twelve months from now.

These laws and principles work. They have worked for thousands of years and they are available to everyone who is willing to apply them.

Throughout the process of writing this book, I applied the thirteen laws. Today you hold it in your hands. On the back of the book cover and in the first few pages of the book, there are a dozen endorsements by high achievers. Most of them I did not know personally. Yet, as I completed the final touches of this project, I set a goal to have these well-known authors make a few remarks regarding this book. Even I was initially surprised, yet accepting when comments came back like, "TJ, you have written a living classic. A symphony of success set to words."

Evidence once again that application of the thirteen laws results in achievement. I specifically knew what I wanted. I imagined in advance, successfully receiving endorsements by these very high achievers. Once I made a definite commitment to complete this book, I immediately took action. I then, confidently asked for endorsements, and I persevered until the goal materialized.

As you read the book over and over, it will begin impacting your thoughts and beliefs, thereby positively impacting your performance. As a result, both large and small goals will materialize into reality. You will be amazed by the power of these simple truths as you read and apply them.

I leave you now, but I pass on to you the same advice once given to me, "May the best of your past, be the worst of your future." Make your future the best that it could possibly be, because it is possible!

The end—*is really the beginning*!

About the Author

TJ HOISINGTON is the founder of Hoisington Leadership International, an organization dedicated to helping individuals and organizations reach their unlimited potential.

TJ Hoisington began his efforts at age sixteen when he discovered his life's purpose was to help people take control of their lives. Using the concepts he teaches, he formed his first company at sixteen and sold it two years later. Later, he was instrumental in starting two companies that both quickly became multi million-dollar corporations.

TJ has advised, addressed, or consulted with corporations such as, Seattle's Best Coffee, Century21, NBC, Toyota, Prudential, Ramada Inn, Pre-Paid Legal Services, Inc, and many more, including schools and non-profit organizations. His ability to help individuals and organizations tap their greatness and potential is extraordinary.

He is the author of several audio programs, including *The Power to Shape Your Life, Achieving Success in Sales, and Inspirational Thoughts, Insights and Truths.*

TJ Hoisington currently resides in Washington State with his wife and two sons.

Acknowledgements

A special thanks to the following individuals who have in their own ways contributed to this book. I sincerely thank each of them for their time and insight that helped make this book a reality.

Thank you, Bob Moawad for your wisdom and understanding of the principles shared in this book. You were an amazing help. I am very thankful to Dick Anderson for the kind support he has given me over the years—starting at age sixteen. A special thanks to a good friend—John Richter. I met John while working for Anthony Robbins and his insights have been brilliant. Thank you Randy Vawdrey for being a wonderful visionary and conceptual thinker. Tom Meagher you are definitely a rising star. You have amazing abilities for detail and a great understanding of grammar, punctuation, spelling, and flow of content. I wouldn't dare forget Hilary Turner, Linda Avery, and Betty Child—I appreciate your editing skills. Thank you Mary Ann Jackson for your understanding and critical eye—it was just what I needed. I have also appreciated your creative mind. I thank my brother Steve Hoisington, who reviewed the manuscript and gave suggestions that enhanced the quality of this book. Lastly, a special thanks to all those who kindly endorsed this book. I have definitely been blessed.

"It's Possible!"